ETHNIC
CONFLICT

Other Books in the At Issue Series:

ETHNIC CONFLICT

David Bender, *Publisher*
Bruno Leone, *Executive Editor*

Katie de Koster, *Managing Editor*
Scott Barbour, *Series Editor*

Charles P. Cozic, *Book Editor*

AT ISSUE

An Opposing Viewpoints Series®

Greenhaven Press, Inc.
San Diego, California

Library of Congress Cataloging-in-Publication Data

At issue: ethnic conflict / editor, Charles Cozic.
    p.   cm. — (At issue series)
  Includes bibliographical references and index.
  ISBN 1-56510-265-7 (pbk.) — ISBN 1-56510-298-3 (lib.).
  1. United States—Race relations. 2. United States—Ethnic relations.
I. Cozic, Charles P., 1957-   . II. Title: Ethnic conflict. III. Series.
E184.A1.A785   1995   94-28349
305.8′00973—dc20   CIP
                                                                   AC

© 1995 by Greenhaven Press, Inc., PO Box 289009,
San Diego, CA 92198-9009

Printed in the U.S.A.

Table of Contents

Introduction

America has long been identified by many people as a predominantly white nation, built on European traditions and Judeo-Christian values. Indeed, the nation's founders considered their Euro-American heritage—and assimilation into it—so important that they drafted a constitutional five-year residency requirement for immigrants seeking citizenship. According to historian Arthur Mann, this requirement "was judged sufficient for immigrants to familiarize themselves with American life."

Throughout America's history, such designs and hopes for assimilation—incorporating different groups into a "melting pot" of one culture, or "monoculture"—became reality. For more than two centuries, the typical American immigrant was white and European: English, Germans, Italians, Eastern Europeans, and others who constituted the first waves of immigration. Such immigrants, though often resented as foreigners and rarely coexisting in total harmony, eventually shed the ties to their homelands in favor of "becoming" American.

But the image of white America perceived by many people is vanishing. Recent immigrant influxes comprising mostly nonwhites such as Asians and Hispanics, as well as increases in America's resident minority populations, are contributing to the so-called "browning" of America. For example, between 1980 and 1990, the nation's Hispanic population increased 53 percent to 22.3 million while the number of Asians more than doubled to 7.3 million. Much of this growth came from immigration. The U.S. Census Bureau reports that during that period 8.6 million immigrants entered the country—the most in eight decades. This rate shows no sign of slowing. According to the Center for Immigration Studies, approximately one million legal and three hundred thousand illegal immigrants now enter the United States annually.

Ethnic conflict: whites vs. others

Many experts argue that nonwhites are on the verge of becoming the majority in California. Former presidential candidate Pat Buchanan has predicted that by 2050 whites may be "near a minority" in America itself. Buchanan warns that such an outcome could raise what he contends are already escalating racial tensions to such levels as experienced in ethnically torn South Africa and the former Yugoslavia. Whether or not this occurs, presently few places in America can claim to be free of ethnic conflict. Large cities such as New York and Los Angeles have historically been, and still are, destinations for immigrants from many different countries. Consequently, discrimination and ethnic tensions have long simmered there, contributing to impoverished ghettos, "white flight" to suburbs, and racial violence. But many newly arrived immigrants today make their homes in smaller cities such as Wausau, Wisconsin, and rural areas that had previously been monoculturally white. As with America's first waves of immigrants, these groups often face similar resentment as foreigners.

In 1980, the Census Bureau found Wausau, now a city of 37,500, to be the most ethnically homogenous U.S. city: less than one percent of residents were nonwhite. But by 1994, children of Southeast Asian refugee families totaled one-fourth of elementary school enrollment, according to writer Roy Beck, who visited Wausau and found what he considered growing tension between native whites and Asians. Writes Beck, "Frustration [among poor refugees], in combination with resentment among natives . . . , seems to be the cause of inter-ethnic violence among the young."

The ethnic discord afflicting large cities had apparently taken root in Wausau—particularly in its schools. According to Beck, many established residents objected to the busing of refugee children and the decline of spoken English in schools, and were shocked by racially motivated youth violence. Voiced one senior school board member, "Immigration has inspired racism here that I never thought we had." Of course, Wausau's immigrants alone did not cause such problems. In fact, Beck writes, "Most residents spoke well of the immigrants as individuals," though "the overwhelming emotion seemed to be" dismay toward the rapid, startling social change transforming their small city.

The multiculturalism controversy

Americans wishing to preserve a monoculture may share similar feelings. What they fear, perhaps more than the sheer increase of minority populations, is the notion of multiculturalism—an emphasis on the different cultural components within a society—and the controversy it has created in schools and elsewhere. According to historian Paul Robeson Jr., "The controversy over multiculturalism . . . is at the heart of a profound ideological struggle over the values of American culture and the nature of U.S. civilization," a struggle between the "monocultural melting pot" and the "multiracial mosaic." Though many monoculturalists tolerate—even welcome—immigrants as long as they assimilate into mainstream culture, they oppose multiculturalism as ideological and cultural heresy.

Multiculturalism takes many diverse forms—from the study of disparate world cultures in schools to bilingualism and multilingualism in communities and government. Proponents of multiculturalism argue that by preaching assimilation and the doctrine of "from the many, one," America has traditionally ignored the richness of other cultures. In the words of professors Gerald Pine and Asa Hilliard, "Through the omission of information, America's schools have become monocultural environments. They dispense a curriculum . . . [that] reinforces institutional racism by excluding from discourse . . . the intellectual thought, scholarship, history, culture, contributions, and experience of minority groups." These and other multiculturalists hold that minority children will better succeed academically by being exposed to, and taking pride in, their various ancestral cultures instead of traditional teaching from a white Eurocentric perspective.

However, opponents contend that multicultural education, which they often deem racist itself, breeds ethnic "tribalism"—a splintering that stresses difference rather than unity. In the words of Arthur Schlesinger Jr., one of the most staunch opponents of multiculturalism, "Militant multiculturalism glorifies ethnic and racial communities at the expense of the common culture. It glorifies ethnic and racial myths at the expense of honest history . . . [and] promotes fragmentation, segregation, ghettoization—all the more dangerous at a time when ethnic conflict is tearing apart one nation after another."

Conflict among minorities

Since America's inception, ethnic conflict has periodically embroiled whites and minorities. While ethnic conflict involving whites against blacks and other minorities—from slavery to the modern civil rights struggle—is a familiar part of American history, conflicts also occur between different minority groups. In 1993, a survey headed by pollster Lou Harris determined that many Asians, blacks, and Hispanics agreed with negative stereotypes of members of other minorities (as well as of whites). In the poll, many blacks and Hispanics regarded Asians as "crafty and devious"; blacks and Asians responded that Hispanics had "bigger families than they were able to support"; and Asians and Hispanics believed that blacks "want to live on welfare."

Such antipathy, along with other factors such as economic decline and competition for jobs in inner cities, may explain recent episodes of urban violence between minority groups. In Los Angeles and many other large cities, the Asian-black-Hispanic combination composes the core of the minority population. In 1992, widespread rioting in Los Angeles evinced stark images of interethnic violence. Then, some inner-city blacks looted or burned scores of Korean-owned businesses. On one side, many blacks claimed that such businesses, including liquor stores, exploited black communities, in part through high retail prices. On the other, Koreans countered that these business owners were merely trying to support, and make better lives for, themselves.

Few cities, if any, are immune from conflict among minorities. According to New York City residents Darryl Powell and Emily Woo Yamasaki:

> In recent years, incidents of mistrust, race-baiting and violence have erupted between U.S. or Caribbean Blacks and Koreans, Vietnamese, and other Asian and Pacific Islander groups from L.A. to Boston. Why? Are our cultures so incompatible that we inevitably clash? Are our people natural racists and xenophobes? We don't believe it.

In 1994, the passage of California's Proposition 187 exposed an altogether different type of ethnic conflict—intraethnic conflict—that affects not only California, but other states and large cities, too. The proposition (legally challenged immediately after its passage) called for the denial of many social services such as education, nonemergency health care, and welfare to illegal immigrants and their children. Many who supported the proposition were legal immigrants, including Hispanics, who protested that while they had entered the country legally and obeyed the laws of the land, illegals (predominantly Hispanic) were breaking the law to take advantage of social services.

Suggestions to cap all these brewing conflicts within, between, and among ethnic groups are many: from championing the melting pot concept and appealing for personal responsibility to advocating acceptance of different cultural points of view and giving minorities better economic opportunities. These recommendations and others are offered by the authors in *At Issue: Ethnic Conflict* as they discuss how Americans should reconcile their ethnic heritages, similarities, and differences.

1

America's Ethnic Conflicts: An Overview

Ronald A. Taylor

Ronald A. Taylor is a reporter for the Washington Times, *a daily newspaper.*

Despite the civil rights movement and America's image as a melting pot, ethnic conflict is on the rise. White opposition to racial preferences and an influx of minority immigrants have strained race relations in many regions, particularly Southern California. There, racial confrontation is commonplace among a mixture of ethnic groups—blacks, Hispanics, Koreans, and others. Racial tension nationwide is compounded by economic woes and a lack of knowledge of other minority groups.

Nearly 30 years after Martin Luther King Jr. evoked it, his vision of universal brotherhood and tolerance remains unfulfilled.

For a nation commonly characterized as a melting pot of nationalities and cultures, the lofty but seemingly attainable goal appeared to be a good idea at the time.

Three decades later, even with slavery, segregation and much of the legal foundation of racism in ruins, the dream that helped earn the 1964 Nobel Peace Prize for Dr. King is still not achieved.

"On a scale of one to 10, we are at about 4.5," said Bruce Anthony Jones, a University of Pittsburgh historian who teaches "Issues of Race and Racism in Society and Education."

Instead, the nation remains a racial battleground. Pressure is building from whites for an end to race-based decision making in the workplace and other areas of life.

Meanwhile, the melting pot has become a cauldron. The nation's population is more diverse—and less white—than ever. It is also teeming with intra-minority racial tensions.

"America is finding that it needs to do more than just throw all the groups under one roof," Mr. Jones said.

"In the middle of an economic downturn and while our society is rapidly undergoing demographic changes and our institutions are not up to speed about educating people and accommodating change, there is a

Ronald A. Taylor, "The Multicultural Melting Pot," *The Washington Times*, January 19, 1992. Reprinted by permission of The Washington Times Corporation.

lot of friction," said Stewart Kwoh, executive director of the Asian Pacific American Legal Center of Southern California.

The center is an umbrella organization for programs to serve the needs of Asian-Americans in that region. The diverse nature of that booming community of immigrants is underscored by the 20 Pacific Rim languages spoken in the southern California area.

As newcomers surged into the region, center officials said, it was inevitable there would be clashes involving the newest wave of hyphenated Americans.

"Culturally, Americans have always been very arrogant and have never been very tolerant," said Marcia Choo, director of the center's mediation services, one of 11 dispute resolution programs for non-violent, out-of-court settlements in Los Angeles County.

Culturally, Americans have always been very arrogant and have never been very tolerant.

Tensions are compounded by the nation's economic woes, she said. "Newcomers are a convenient target or scapegoat.

"Immigrants are always an easy target. They don't speak the language, and the culture is different from what people who were born here are used to."

For the Asian and Hispanic communities, the experiences of recent years have mirrored a racial insensitivity that led to riots and other civil disturbances in black urban communities during the 1960s and 1970s.

The Adams Morgan and Mount Pleasant communities [in Washington, D.C., experienced] rioting in 1991 that focused Mayor Sharon Pratt Kelly's attention on the Hispanic community's problems and complaints.

Southern California has been wrestling with similar problems among Asian newcomers there.

A multi-ethnic coalition was formed in the San Gabriel Valley in 1991 after fighting erupted between Latino and Asian students at San Gabriel High.

Ms. Choo has been working with Compton city officials on a community relations plan to recruit more Samoan residents for city services jobs. That grew out of efforts to quell complaints from Pacific Rim immigrants after two Samoans were shot to death in a clash with police.

Black-Korean conflict

Yet fierce intra-minority warfare has occurred between blacks and Korean merchants, many of whom operate in predominantly black neighborhoods.

Korean-American merchants now refuse to sell a malt beer called St. Ides because it is promoted by a black rap musician who has written a song that threatens Korean shopkeepers in black neighborhoods.

In a song by rapper Ice Cube, Korean merchants are told either to treat black customers with more respect or "We'll burn your store right down to a crisp."

The song followed the 1991 death of 15-year-old Latasha Harlins, who died of gunshot wounds inside a Korean-owned supermarket in Los Angeles after being accused of shoplifting a $1.79 bottle of orange juice.

Soon Ja Du, the Korean grocer, received probation for the shooting and the resulting howls from the black community focused fresh attention on complaints that Asian merchants fail to show respect to black customers.

"One reason for the clash is that both communities are really ignorant of the other" Ms. Choo said.

"Blacks see them coming in, buying up businesses in their communities. There is even a conspiracy theory that the Korean government gives them money to come in and take over," she said.

At the same time, she said, Korean newcomers are unaware that blacks played a key role in establishing the rights and opportunities that make the United States so attractive to immigrants.

"The Koreans who have just gotten here are not aware of the civil rights movement," said Ms. Choo, a 27-year-old born in Seoul and brought to this country as a 5-year-old.

"They don't realize that the reason they can send their children to the best schools is that blacks died for the right."

Blacks in urban areas complain that the conventional wisdom that the newest immigrant group replaces its predecessor at the bottom of the socio-economic ladder is inoperative when it comes to blacks.

"The Koreans listened to Louis Farrakhan and the blacks didn't," said the Rev. Raymond Kemp, pastor of Holy Comforter-St. Cyprian Catholic Church in Washington. "Koreans decided to build from the corner up."

Other groups

Meanwhile, population gains by other minorities threaten to push aside blacks as the nation's dominant minority.

During the 1980s, while the white population was in relative decline, the Hispanic population increased more than 50 percent and the Asian-American proportion of the U.S. population rose to 3 percent.

The growing minority populations coincided with a rise in hate crimes and racially linked acts of violence, according to Justice Department figures.

Mr. Jones said the pace toward achievement of King's dream has slowed, in part because of racial insecurities heightened by anxieties over the U.S. economic downturn.

Such insecurities are fueled by the messages of such people as former Ku Klux Klan member David Duke and City College of New York Professor Leonard Jeffries.

Both men have built small but vocal followings by preaching racial superiority.

Integration, the primary vehicle for achieving a color-blind society, is now viewed by many as unworkable.

Population gains by other minorities threaten to push aside blacks as the nation's dominant minority.

Even the word integration is in disrepute these days, said Earlham College President Richard Wood, a veteran of sit-ins and marches of the civil rights movement in the 1960s.

"It's interesting. You hardly ever hear the word anymore, except in a derisive way," Mr. Wood said. "Integration was supposed to mean the elimination of separate but unequal treatment of minority Americans. It meant that we would try to be a color-blind society."

Now, he said, "there is a real struggle about whether we all want to be participants in a common American culture with some variety, or if we want to emphasize our differences."

At any rate, blacks and whites are not the only combatants on the battlefields of what has become a 30 years' war against racism.

2

The Value of Immigrants

Francis Fukuyama

Francis Fukuyama is a former deputy director of the U.S. State Department's policy planning staff. He is currently a resident consultant at the Washington, D.C., office of the RAND Corporation, a think tank. Fukuyama is the author of The End of History and the Last Man, *a best-selling book about the demise of communism and the prevalence of democracy.*

The vast majority of non-European immigrants do not bear undesirable cultural values and are not the enemy of American culture. Many such immigrants possess strong work and family values. America should not keep newcomers out, but should encourage immigrants to absorb American language and rules. Multiculturalism, an American invention, is not necessary to assimilate them. Early immigrants, such as Italians and Poles who arrived in America early in the twentieth century, assimilated themselves easily without public celebration of their native cultures. Although immigration is the source of major economic and social problems, America's cultural breakdown has not been caused by immigrants, but by capitalism, divorce, feminism, technological change, and other factors, all of which originated within America's white Anglo-Saxon communities.

At the 1992 Republican convention in Houston, Patrick J. Buchanan announced the coming of a block-by-block war to "take back our culture." Buchanan is right that a cultural war is upon us, and that this fight will be a central American preoccupation now that the cold war is over. What he understands less well, however, is that the vast majority of the non-European immigrants who have come into this country in the past couple of decades are not the enemy. Indeed, many of them are potentially on his side.

Conservatives have for long been sharply divided on the question of immigration. Many employers and proponents of free-market economics, like Julian Simon or the editorial page of the *Wall Street Journal*, are strongly pro-immigration; they argue for open borders because immigrants are a source of cheap labor and ultimately create more wealth than they consume. Buchanan and other traditional right-wing Republicans, by contrast, represent an older nativist position. They dispute the eco-

Francis Fukuyama, "Immigrants and Family Values." Reprinted from *Commentary*, May 1993, by permission; all rights reserved.

nomic benefits of immigration, but more importantly look upon immigrants as bearers of foreign and less desirable cultural values. It is this group of conservatives who forced the inclusion of a plank in the Republican platform calling for the creation of "structures" to maintain the integrity of America's southern border.

Indeed, hostility to immigration has made for peculiar bedfellows. The Clinton administration's difficulties in finding an attorney general who had not at some point hired an illegal-immigrant babysitter is testimony to the objective dependence of liberal yuppies on immigration to maintain their life-styles, and they by and large would support the *Wall Street Journal*'s open-borders position.

The symptoms of cultural decay are all around us, but the last people in the world we should be blaming are recent immigrants.

On the other hand, several parts of the liberal coalition—blacks and environmentalists—have been increasingly vocal in recent years in opposition to further immigration, particularly from Latin America. The Black Leadership Forum, headed by Coretta Scott King and Congressman Walter Fauntroy, has lobbied to maintain sanctions against employers hiring illegal immigrant labor on the ground that this takes away jobs from blacks and "legal" browns. Jack Miles, a former *Los Angeles Times* book-review editor with impeccable liberal credentials, has in [an October 1992] article in the *Atlantic* lined up with the Federation for American Immigration Reform (FAIR) in calling for a rethinking of open borders, while liberal activist groups like the Southern California Interfaith Task Force on Central America have supported Senator Orrin Hatch's legislation strengthening employer sanctions. Environmental groups like the Sierra Club, for their part, oppose immigration because it necessitates economic growth, use of natural resources, and therefore environmental degradation.

But if much of the liberal opposition to immigration has focused on economic issues, the conservative opposition has concentrated on the deeper cultural question; and here the arguments made by the Right are very confused. The symptoms of cultural decay are all around us, but the last people in the world we should be blaming are recent immigrants.

Culture and assimilation

The most articulate and reasoned recent conservative attack on immigration came in [a June 22, 1992] article in *National Review* by Peter Brimelow. Brimelow, a senior editor at *Forbes* and himself a naturalized American of British and Canadian background, argues that immigration worked in the past in America only because earlier waves of nativist backlash succeeded in limiting it to a level that could be successfully assimilated into the dominant Anglo-Saxon American culture. Brimelow criticizes pro-immigration free-marketeers like Julian Simon for ignoring the issue of the skill levels of the immigrant labor force, and their likely impact on blacks and others at the bottom end of the economic ladder. But his basic complaint is a cultural one. Attacking the *Wall Street Journal*'s Paul Gigot for remarking that a million Zulus would probably work harder than a million Englishmen today, Brimelow notes:

> This comment reveals an utter innocence about the reality of ethnic and cultural differences, let alone little things like tradition and history—in short, the greater part of the conservative vision. Even in its own purblind terms, it is totally false. All the empirical evidence is that immigrants from developed countries assimilate better than those from underdeveloped countries. It is developed countries that teach the skills required for success in the United States . . . it should not be necessary to explain that the legacy of [the Zulu kings] Shaka and Cetewayo—overthrown just over a century ago—is not that of Alfred the Great, let alone Elizabeth II or any civilized society.

Elsewhere, Brimelow suggests that culture is a key determinant of economic performance, and that people from certain cultures are therefore likely to do less well economically than others. He implies, furthermore, that some immigrants are more prone to random street crime because of their "impulsiveness and present-orientation," while others are responsible for organized crime which is, by his account, ethnically based. Finally, Brimelow argues that the arrival of diverse non-European cultures fosters the present atmosphere of multiculturalism, and is, to boot, bad for the electoral prospects of the Republican party.

A similar line of thought runs through Buchanan's writings and speeches, and leads to a similar anti-immigrant posture. Buchanan has explicitly attacked the notion that democracy represents a particularly positive form of government, and hence would deny that belief in universal democratic principles ought to be at the core of the American national identity.[1] But if one subtracts democracy from American nationality, what is left? Apparently, though Buchanan is somewhat less explicit on this point, a concept of America as a Christian, ethnically European nation with certain core cultural values that are threatened by those coming from other cultures and civilizations.

Immigrants are likely to be a self-selecting group with a much greater than average degree of energy, ambition, toughness, and adaptability.

There is an easy, Civics 101-type answer to the Brimelow-Buchanan argument. In contrast to other West European democracies, or Japan, the American national identity has never been directly linked to ethnicity or religion. Nationality has been based instead on universal concepts like freedom and equality that are in theory open to all people. Our Constitution forbids the establishment of religion, and the legal system has traditionally held ethnicity at arm's length. To be an American has meant to be committed to a certain set of ideas, and not to be descended from an original tribe of *ur*-Americans. Those elements of a common American culture visible today—belief in the Constitution and the individualist-egalitarian principles underlying it, plus modern American pop and consumer culture—are universally accessible and appealing, making the United States, in Ben Wattenberg's phrase, the first "universal nation."

This argument is correct as far as it goes, but there is a serious counterargument that reaches to the core of 1992's debate over "family values." It runs as follows:

America began living up to its universalist principles only in the last half of this century. For most of the period from its revolutionary founding to its rise as a great, modern, industrial power, the nation's elites conceived of the country not just as a democracy based on universal principles, but also as a Christian, Anglo-Saxon nation.

American democracy—the counterargument continues—is, of course, embodied in the laws and institutions of the country, and will be imbibed by anyone who learns to play by its rules. But virtually every serious theorist of American democracy has noted that its success depended heavily on the presence of certain pre-democratic values or cultural characteristics that were neither officially sanctioned nor embodied in law. If the Declaration of Independence and the Constitution were the basis of America's *Gesellschaft* (society), Christian Anglo-Saxon culture constituted its *Gemeinschaft* (community).

Indeed—the counterargument goes on—the civic institutions that Tocqueville observed in the 1830's, whose strength and vitality he saw as a critical manifestation of the Americans' "art of associating," were more often than not of a religious (i.e., Christian) nature, devoted to temperance, moral education of the young, or the abolition of slavery. There is nothing in the Constitution which states that parents should make large sacrifices for their children, that workers should rise early in the morning and labor long hours in order to get ahead, that people should emulate rather than undermine their neighbors' success, that they should be innovative, entrepreneurial, or open to technological change. Yet Americans, formed by a Christian culture, possessed these traits in abundance for much of their history, and the country's economic prosperity and social cohesion arguably rested on them.

The family-values issue

It is this sort of consideration that underlay the family-values controversy during the 1992 election. Basic to this line of thought is that, all other things being equal, children are better off when raised in stable, two-parent, heterosexual families. Such family structures and the web of moral obligations they entail are the foundation of educational achievement, economic success, good citizenship, personal character, and a host of other social virtues.

The issue of family values was badly mishandled by the Republicans and deliberately misconstrued by the press and the Democrats (often not distinguishable), such that mere mention of the phrase provoked derisive charges of narrow-minded gay-bashing and hostility to single mothers. Yet while many Americans did not sign on to 1992's family-values theme, few would deny that the family and community are in deep crisis today. The breakdown of the black family in inner-city neighborhoods around America in the past couple of generations shows in particularly stark form the societal consequences of a loss of certain cultural values. And what has happened among blacks is only an extreme extension of a process that has been proceeding apace among whites as well.

The issue, then, is not whether the questions of culture and cultural values are important, or whether it is legitimate to raise them, but whether immigration really threatens those values. For while the values one might deem central either to economic success or to social cohesion may have arisen out of a Christian, Anglo-Saxon culture, it is clear that they are not bound to that particular social group: some groups, like Jews and Asians, might come to possess those values in abundance, while Wasps themselves might lose them and decay. The question thus becomes: which ethnic groups in today's America are threatening, and which groups are promoting, these core cultural values?

The notion that non-European immigrants are a threat to family values and other core American cultural characteristics is, in a way, quite puzzling. After all, the breakdown of traditional family structures, from extended to nuclear, has long been understood to be a disease of advanced industrial countries and not of nations just emerging from their agricultural pasts.

Some conservatives tend to see the third world as a vast, global underclass, teeming with the same social pathologies as Compton in Los Angeles or Bedford-Stuyvesant in Brooklyn. But the sad fact is that the decay of basic social relationships evident in American inner cities, stretching to the most intimate moral bonds linking parents and children, may well be something with few precedents in human history. Economic conditions in most third-world countries simply would not permit a social group suffering so total a collapse of family structure to survive: with absent fathers and no source of income, or mothers addicted to drugs, children would not live to adulthood.

But it would also seem *a priori* likely that third-world immigrants should have stronger family values than white, middle-class, suburban Americans, while their work ethic and willingness to defer to traditional sources of authority should be greater as well. Few of the factors that have led to family breakdown in the American middle class over the past couple of generations—rapidly changing economic conditions, with their attendant social disruptions; the rise of feminism and the refusal of women to play traditional social roles; or the legitimization of alternative lifestyles and consequent proliferation of rights and entitlements on a retail level—apply in third-world situations. Immigrants coming from traditional developing societies are likely to be poorer, less educated, and in possession of fewer skills than those from Europe, but they are also likely to have stronger family structures and moral inhibitions. Moreover, despite the greater ease of moving to America today than in the last century, immigrants are likely to be a self-selecting group with a much greater than average degree of energy, ambition, toughness, and adaptability.

The real danger is not that . . . elites will become corrupted by the habits and practices of third-world immigrants, but rather that the immigrants will become corrupted by them.

These intuitions are largely borne out by the available empirical data, particularly if one disaggregates the different parts of the immigrant community.

The strength of traditional family values is most evident among immigrants from East and South Asia, where mutually supportive family structures have long been credited as the basis for their economic success. According to Census Bureau statistics, 78 percent of Asian and Pacific Islander households in the United States were family households, as opposed to 70 percent for white Americans. The size of these family households is likely to be larger: 74 percent consist of three or more persons, compared to 57 percent for white families. While Asians are equally likely to be married as whites, they are only half as likely to be divorced.[2] Though dropping off substantially in the second and third generations, concern for elderly parents is high in Chinese, Japanese, and Vietnamese households; for many, the thought of sticking a mother or father out of sight and out of mind in a nursing home continues to be anathema. More importantly, most of the major Asian immigrant groups are intent on rapid assimilation into the American mainstream, and have not been particularly vocal in pressing for particularistic cultural entitlements.

Latinos: A devotion to work and family

While most white Americans are ready to recognize and celebrate the social strengths of Asians, the real fears of cultural invasion surround Latinos. Despite their fast growth, Asians still constitute less than 3 percent of the U.S. population, while the number of Hispanics increased from 14.6 to over 22 million between 1980 and 1990, or 9 percent of the population. But here as well, the evidence suggests that most Latin American immigrants may be a source of strength with regard to family values, and not a liability.

Latinos today constitute an extremely diverse group. It is certainly the case that a segment of the Latino community has experienced many of the same social problems as blacks. This is particularly true of the first large Latino community in the U.S.: Puerto Ricans who came to the mainland in the early postwar period and settled predominantly in New York and other cities of the Northeast. Forty percent of Puerto Rican families are headed by women, compared to 16 percent for the non-Hispanic population; only 57 percent of Puerto Rican households consist of families, while their rate of out-of-wedlock births is almost double the rate for non-Hispanics. In New York, Puerto Ricans have re-exported social pathologies like crack-cocaine use to Puerto Rico over the past generation.

Other Latino groups have also brought social problems with them: the Mariel boat lift from Cuba, during which Castro emptied his country's jails and insane asylums, had a measurable impact on crime in the U.S. Many war-hardened immigrants from El Salvador and other unstable Central American countries have contributed to crime in the U.S., and Chicano gangs in Los Angeles and other Southwestern cities have achieved their own notoriety beside the black Bloods and Crips. Half of those arrested in the 1992 Los Angeles riot were Latinos.

Such facts are highly visible and contribute to the impression among white Americans that Latinos as a whole have joined inner-city blacks to form one vast, threatening underclass. But there are very significant differences among Latino groups. Latinos of Cuban and Mexican origin, for example, who together constitute 65 percent of the Hispanic community, have a 50-percent lower rate of female-headed households than do Puerto Ricans—18.9 and 19.6 percent versus 38.9 percent. While the rate of Puerto Rican out-of-wedlock births approaches that of blacks (53.0 vs. 63.1 percent of live births), the rates for Cuban and Mexican-origin Latinos are much lower, 16.1 and 28.9 percent, respectively, though they are still above the white rate of 13.9 percent.[3]

When looked at in the aggregate, Latino family structure stands somewhere between that of whites and blacks. For example, the rates of female-headed families with no husband present as a proportion of total families is 13.5 percent for whites, 46.4 percent for blacks, and 24.4 percent for Hispanics. If we adjust these figures for income level, however, Hispanics turn out to be much closer to the white norm.

Poverty is hard on families regardless of race; part of the reason for the higher percentage of Latino female-headed households is simply that there are more poor Latino families. If we compare families below the poverty level, the Hispanic rate of female-headed families is very close to that of whites (45.7 vs. 43.6 percent), while the comparable rate for blacks is much higher than either (78.3 percent). Considering the substantially higher rate of family breakdown within the sizable Puerto Rican community, this suggests that the rate of single-parent families for Cuban- and Mexican-origin Latinos is actually lower than that for whites at a comparable income level.

Moreover, Latinos as a group are somewhat more likely to be members of families than either whites or blacks.[4] Another study indicates that Mexican-Americans have better family demographics than do whites, with higher birth-weight babies even among low-income mothers due to taboos on smoking, drinking, and drug use during pregnancy. Many Latinos remain devout Catholics, and the rate of church attendance is higher in the Mexican community than for the U.S. as a whole as well. But even if one does not believe that the United States is a "Christian country," the fact that so many immigrants are from Catholic Latin America should make them far easier to assimilate than, say, Muslims in Europe.

These statistics are broadly in accord with the observations of anyone who has lived in Los Angeles, San Diego, or any other community in the American Southwest. Virtually every early-morning commuter in Los Angeles knows the streetcorners on which Chicano day-laborers gather at 7:00 A.M., looking for work as gardeners, busboys, or on construction sites. Many of them are illegal immigrants with families back in Mexico to whom they send their earnings. While they are poor and unskilled, they have a work ethic and devotion to family comparable to those of the South and East European immigrants who came to the U.S. at the turn of the century. It is much less common to see African-Americans doing this sort of thing.

Cultural breakdown

Those who fear third-world immigration as a threat to Anglo-American cultural values do not seem to have noticed what the real sources of cultural breakdown have been. To some extent, they can be traced to broad socioeconomic factors over which none of us has control: the fluid, socially disruptive nature of capitalism; technological change; economic pressures of the contemporary workplace and urban life; and so on. But the ideological assault on traditional family values—the sexual revolution; feminism and the delegitimization of the male-dominated household; the celebration of alternative life-styles; attempts ruthlessly to secularize all aspects of American public life; the acceptance of no-fault divorce and the consequent rise of single-parent households—was not the creation of recently-arrived Chicano agricultural workers or Haitian boat people, much less of Chinese or Korean immigrants. They originated right in the heart of America's well-established white, Anglo-Saxon community. The "Hollywood elite" that created the now celebrated Murphy Brown, much like the establishment "media elite" that Republicans enjoy attacking, does not represent either the values or the interests of most recent third-world immigrants.

In short, though the old, traditional culture continues to exist in the United States, it is overlaid today with an elite culture that espouses very different values. The real danger is not that these elites will become corrupted by the habits and practices of third-world immigrants, but rather that the immigrants will become corrupted by them. And that is in fact what tends to happen.

While the first generation of immigrants to the United States tends to be deferential to established authority and preoccupied with the economic problems of "making it," their children and grandchildren become aware of their own entitlements and rights, more politicized, and able to exploit the political system to defend and expand those entitlements. While the first generation is willing to work quietly at minimum- or subminimum-wage jobs, the second and third generations have higher expectations as to what their labor is worth. The extension of welfare and other social benefits to noncitizens through a series of court decisions has had the perverse effect of hastening the spread of welfare dependency. Part of the reason that Puerto Ricans do less well than other Latino groups may be that they were never really immigrants at all, but U.S. citizens, and therefore eligible for social benefits at a very early stage.

As Julian Simon has shown, neither the absolute nor the relative levels of immigration over the past decade have been inordinately high by historical standards. What *is* different and very troubling about immigration in the present period is that the ideology that existed at the turn of the century and promoted assimilation into the dominant Anglo-Saxon culture has been replaced by a multicultural one that legitimates and even promotes continuing cultural differentness.

The multicultural curriculum

The intellectual and social origins of multiculturalism are complex, but one thing is clear: it is both a Western and an American invention. The American Founding was based on certain Enlightenment notions of the universality of human equality and freedom, but such ideas have been under attack within the Western tradition itself for much of the past two centuries. The second half of the late Allan Bloom's *The Closing of the American Mind* (the part that most buyers of the book skipped over) chronicles the way in which the relativist ideas of [German philosophers] Friedrich Nietzsche and Martin Heidegger were transported to American shores at mid-century. Combined with an easygoing American egalitarianism, they led not just to a belief in the need for cultural tolerance, but to a positive assertion of the equal moral validity of all cultures. Today the writings of Michel Foucault, a French epigone of Nietzsche, have become the highbrow source of academic multiculturalism.

France may have produced Foucault, but France has not implemented a multicultural educational curriculum to anything like the degree the U.S. has. The origins of multiculturalism here must therefore be traced to the specific circumstances of American social life. Contrary to the arguments of multiculturalism's promoters, it was not a necessary adjustment to the reality of our pluralistic society. The New York City public-school system in the year 1910 was as diverse as it is today, and yet it never occurred to anyone to celebrate and preserve the native cultures of the city's Italians, Greeks, Poles, Jews, or Chinese.

The shift in attitudes toward cultural diversity can be traced to the aftermath of the civil-rights movement, when it became clear that integration was not working for blacks. The failure to assimilate was interpreted as an indictment of the old, traditional mainstream Anglo-Saxon culture: "Wasp" took on a pejorative connotation, and African-Americans began to take pride in the separateness of their own traditions. Ironically, the experience of African-Americans became the model for subsequent immigrant groups like Latinos who could have integrated themselves into mainstream society as easily as the Italians or Poles before them.

Paul Gigot may or may not be right that a million Zulus would work harder than a million English, but a million Taiwanese certainly would.

It is true that Hispanic organizations now constitute part of the multiculturalist coalition and have been very vocal in pushing for bilingual/bicultural education. There is increasing evidence, however, that rank-and-file immigrants are much more traditionally assimilationist than some of their more vocal leaders. For example, most Chinese and Russian immigrant parents in New York City deliberately avoid sending their children to the bilingual-education classes offered to them by the public-school system, believing that a cold plunge into English will be a much more effective means of learning to function in American society.

Hispanics generally show more support for bilingual education, but even here a revealing study indicates that an overwhelming number of Hispanic parents see bilingualism primarily as a means of learning English, and not of preserving Hispanic culture.[5] This same study indicates that most Hispanics identify strongly with the United States, and show a relatively low level of Spanish maintenance in the home. By contrast, multiculturalism is more strongly supported by many other groups— blacks, feminists, gays, Native Americans, etc.—whose ancestors have been in the country from the start.

Brimelow's *National Review* piece suggests that even if immigrants are not responsible for our anti-assimilationist multiculturalism, we need not pour oil on burning waters by letting in more immigrants from non-Western cultures. But this argument can be reversed: even if the rate of new immigration fell to zero tomorrow, and the most recent five million immigrants were sent home, we would still have an enormous problem in this country with the breakdown of a core culture and the infatuation of the school system with trendy multiculturalist educational policies.

The real fight, the central fight, then, should not be over keeping newcomers out: this will be a waste of time and energy. The real fight ought to be over the question of assimilation itself: whether we believe that there is enough to our Western, rational, egalitarian, democratic civilization to force those coming to the country to absorb its language and rules, or whether we carry respect for other cultures to the point that Americans no longer have a common voice with which to speak to one another.

Apart from the humble habits of work and family values, opponents of immigration ought to consider culture at the high end of the scale. As anyone who has walked around an elite American university recently would know, immigration from Asia is transforming the nature of American education. For a country that has long prided itself on technological superiority, and whose economic future rests in large part on a continuing technical edge, a depressingly small number of white Americans from long-established families choose to go into engineering and science programs in preference to business and, above all, law school. (This is particularly true of the most dynamic and vocal part of the white population, upwardly mobile middle-class women.) The one bright spot in an otherwise uniform horizon of decline in educational test scores has been in math, where large numbers of new Asian test-takers have bumped up the numbers.[6] In Silicon Valley alone, there are some 12,000 engineers of Chinese descent, while Chinese account for two out of every five engineering and science graduates in the University of California system.

Indeed, if one were to opt for "designer immigration" that would open the gates to peoples with the best cultural values, it is not at all clear that certain European countries would end up on top.

In the past decade, England's per-capita GNP [gross national product] has fallen behind Italy's, and threatens to displace Portugal and Greece at the bottom of the European Community heap by the end of the decade. Only a fifth of English young people receive any form of higher education, and despite Margaret Thatcher's best efforts, little progress has been made over the past generation in breaking down the stifling social rigidities of the British class system. The English working class is among the least well-educated, most state- and welfare-dependent and immobile of any in the developed world. While the British intelligentsia and upper classes continue to intimidate middle-class Americans, they can do so only on the basis of snobbery and inherited but rapidly dwindling intellectual capital. Paul Gigot may or may not be right that a million Zulus would work harder than a million English, but a million Taiwanese certainly would, and would bring with them much stronger family structures and entrepreneurship to boot.

Problems with immigration

This is not to say that immigration will not be the source of major economic and social problems for the United States in the future. There are at least three areas of particular concern.

The first has to do with the effects of immigration on income distribution, particularly at the low end of the scale. The growing inequality of American income distribution over the past decade is not, as the Democrats asserted during the election campaign, the result of Reagan-Bush tax policies or the failure of "trickle-down" economics. Rather, it proceeds from the globalization of the American economy: low-skill labor increasingly has to compete with low-skill labor in Malaysia, Brazil, Mexico, and elsewhere. But it has also had to compete with low-skill immigrant labor coming into the country from the third world, which explains why Hispanics themselves tend to oppose further Hispanic immigration. The country as a whole may be better off economically as a result of this immigration, but those against whom immigrants directly compete have been hurt, just as they will be hurt by the North American Free Trade

Agreement (NAFTA), the General Agreement on Tariffs and Trade (GATT), and other trade-liberalizing measures that are good for the country as a whole. In a city like Los Angeles, Hispanics with their stronger social ties have displaced blacks out of a variety of menial jobs, adding to the woes of an already troubled black community.

The second problem area has to do with the regional concentration of recent Hispanic immigration. As everyone knows, the 25 million Hispanics in the United States are not evenly distributed throughout the country, but are concentrated in the Southwest portion of it, where the problems normally accompanying the assimilation of immigrant communities tend to be magnified. The L.A. public-school system is currently in a state of breakdown, as it tries to educate burgeoning numbers of recent immigrants on a recession-starved budget.

The third problem concerns bilingualism and the elite Hispanic groups which promote and exist off of it. As noted earlier, the rank-and-file of the Hispanic community seems reasonably committed to assimilation; the same cannot be said for its leadership. Bilingualism, which initially began as a well-intentioned if misguided bridge toward learning English, has become in the eyes of many of its proponents a means of keeping alive a separate Spanish language and culture. Numerous studies have indicated that students in bilingual programs learn English less well than those without access to them, and that their enrollments are swelled by a large number of Hispanics who can already speak English perfectly well.[7] In cities with large Hispanic populations like New York and Los Angeles, the bilingual bureaucracy has become something of a monster, rigidly tracking students despite the wishes of parents and students. The *New York Times* recently reported the case of a Hispanic-surnamed child, born in the United States and speaking only English, who was forced by New York City officials to enroll in an English as a Second Language Class. Bilingualism is but one symptom of a much broader crisis in American public education, and admittedly makes the problems of assimilation much greater.

These problems can be tackled with specific changes in public policy. But the central issue raised by the immigration question is indeed a cultural one, and as such less susceptible of policy manipulation. The problem here is not the foreign culture that immigrants bring with them from the third world, but the contemporary elite culture of Americans—Americans like Kevin Costner, who believes that America began going downhill when the white man set foot here, or another American, Ice-T, whose family has probably been in the country longer than Costner's and who believes that women are bitches and that the chief enemy of his generation is the police. In the upcoming block-by-block cultural war, the enemy will not speak Spanish or have a brown skin. In Pogo's words, "He is us."

Notes

1. See, for example, his article, "America First—and Second, and Third," the *National Interest*, Spring 1990.

2. Census Bureau Press Release CB92-89, "Profile of Asians and Pacific Islanders."

3. Data taken from Linda Chavez, *Out of the Barrio* (Basic Books, 1991), p. 103.

4. Figures taken from *Poverty in the United States: 1991*, Bureau of the Census, Series P-60, no. 181, pp. 7-9; the percentage of people in families for whites, blacks, and Hispanics is 84.5, 84.8, and 89.0, respectively (pp. 2-3).

5. See Rodolfo O. de la Garza, Louis DeSipio, *et al.*, *Latino Voices: Mexican, Puerto Rican, and Cuban Perspectives on American Politics* (Westview Press, 1992).

6. This same group of Asians appears also to have lowered verbal scores, though this is something that will presumably be corrected over time.

7. On this point, see Linda Chavez's *Out of the Barrio*, pp. 9-38.

3

The Threat from Immigrants

James Thornton

James Thornton is a Greek Orthodox priest in Garden Grove, California, and a contributing writer for the New American, *a biweekly conservative magazine.*

The immigration problem lies at the heart of the question as to whether the United States will survive as a free nation over the next decades. The impact of the immigrant invasion on America has strong similarities to the displacement of ancient Romans by non-Romans. In Rome, the responsible, law-abiding citizenry became displaced by freed slaves and pagan cult members who laid waste to a great civilization. In America, Third World immigrants are not assimilating our Greco-Roman-Christian heritage, but altering America to resemble their homelands. Because culture is one of the most powerful forces in the world, we should heed America's Founders, who warned about the hazards of massive immigration by people still devoted to their native values and culture.

Comparisons between the American Republic and the ancient Roman Republic are as old as the foundations of this country, so much so that to some they may seem, at times, almost platitudinous. Yet, the resemblance between the two great historical entities—Rome and America—is so great, and parallels so altogether fitting, that, whatever the outcome of our present difficulties may be, comparisons will be made so long as there are still men competent to reflect on history.

Moreover, the Founders of the United States, as we know, consciously modelled their efforts at statecraft on the experiences of classical Rome, contemplating with great care both the triumphs and the inadequacies of the system fashioned by the ancients. Inasmuch as our forefathers considered such studies crucial to their endeavors, we are wise if we continue to do the same.

In an earlier essay entitled "Crumbling From Within" (*The New American*, November 19, 1991), we explored many aspects of the close analogy between Rome and America, centering especially on economic and taxation policies and on the erosion of morality. Only somewhat lightly did we touch on the problem of immigration. That problem deserves further and more detailed attention, however, since it lies at the very heart of the question as to whether the United States will survive as a free and inde-

James Thornton, "Multicultural Invasion," *The New American*, September 1994. Reprinted with permission.

pendent nation over the next few decades.

The renowned classical scholar, Tenny Frank (1876-1939), professor of Latin and ancient Roman history at Johns Hopkins University, in the final chapter of his superlative volume, A *History of Rome*, examines a number of causes for that Empire's sudden decline. Among other things, Professor Frank identifies the differences that distinguish the citizens of the Republic from those of the deteriorating Empire.

> That calm temper of the old state-builders, their love of law and or-
> der, their persistence in liberal and equitable dealings, in patient
> and untiring effort, their deliberation in reaching decisions, their
> distrust of emotions and intuitions, their unswerving devotion to
> liberty, their loyalty to tradition and to the state are the things one
> expects to find so long as the old Roman families are the dominant
> element in the Republic. By contrast the people of the Empire seem
> subservient and listless, caloric and unsteady, soft of fiber, weak of
> will, mentally fatigued, wont to abandon the guidance of reason
> for a crepuscular mysticism.

Lest the comment about "crepuscular mysticism" cause misunderstanding, we hasten to add that Professor Frank strongly dissents from the opinions of Gibbon and Nietzsche that Christianity contributed to the decline of Rome and instead asserts that "the Christians, through their belief in divine aid and their respect for duty, seem to have developed a vigor and determination that might if anything have revitalized the Empire. . . ." By mysticism Frank refers, doubtless, to the multitudes of strange pagan cults that arose in Rome like fungi on a decaying cadaver, their penetration into the Roman community and the influx of vast hordes of non-Romans, mostly slaves, occurring simultaneously.

Eventually, of course, those slaves became freedmen and finally new citizens. But Romans they became in name only. True, they not infrequently donned the clothes of Romans and, for a time, imitated other outward forms of Roman civilization. Of the inward and profound meanings of those forms, however, the aliens could know absolutely nothing. "Slaves," Professor Frank writes, "displaced the citizens of a race that had made Rome what it was. And however clever, however efficient they might be as individuals, they were Romans neither in tradition nor in temper, and they were all too apt to carry a slave's ideals of conduct into the performance of their new offices as citizens."

Radically different cultures

After addressing a multitude of possible explanations for Rome's decline, from soil exhaustion to various economic factors, Frank concludes his investigation with these words: "If from these many causes of Rome's decline we must select the more potent ones, we should be inclined to name first Rome's rapid and ill-considered expansion, the existence of slavery on a vast scale, and as an immediate consequence of these two, the thorough-going displacement of Romans by non-Romans."

We should remember that Tenny Frank published his *History of Rome* in the early-1920s, when issues such as "multiculturalism" and "cultural pluralism" were still far in the future. Nevertheless, the similarities between Rome, as described by the great historian, and the situation that has arisen during the past three decades in this country, are startling, to say the least.

In one respect the two historical situations differ, in that the incorporation by the Romans of vast alien populations through their astonishing conquests and expansion, beginning in the late republican period, does not precisely resemble the experience of our own country. Although our nation did indeed expand from the Atlantic to the Pacific this did not result in our being overwhelmed by newly incorporated foreigners. The source of our difficulty arises not from the incorporation of peoples already living on the lands that eventually became part of America (except to a comparatively minor degree), but from outside. Considering the relative ease and cheapness of modern travel, and our largely open borders, the ramifications of the two distinct historical circumstances are approximately the same. America is being overwhelmed, as Rome was overwhelmed, by populations permeated with cultures, religions, folkways, ideals of government, and patterns of life radically different from, and often in conflict with, our own.

America is being overwhelmed . . . by populations permeated with cultures . . . and patterns of life radically different from, and often in conflict with, our own.

In most cases Third World populations, by their very nature, are temperamentally different from the European Christians who settled North America, fashioned the United States, devised its system of laws, and fathered its free institutions. For those who doubt that temperament plays any role in these things, I suggest they compare life in Calcutta with that in Edinburgh, Hong Kong with that in Frankfurt, Mogadishu with that in Brussels, or pre-1960 Los Angeles, New York, and Boston with those same cities now. In other cases it is not so much temperament that distinguishes people as it is the persistence of age-old cultures. Beliefs in paternalism and, sometimes, despotism are deeply ingrained in many of the world's cultures, going back millennia, and culture, as we know, is one of the most powerful forces in the world.

When Pat Buchanan stated, a few years ago, that 50,000 Englishmen would adapt more quickly to life in America than 50,000 Zulus, he was stigmatized with words such as "racist" and "fascist." In fact, however, Mr. Buchanan was giving voice to all that we have just noted; the human race is blessed with tremendous variety and not all men are equally fitted to the American way of life. Underscoring these truths, the conservative essayist and *Chronicles* editor, Thomas Fleming, writes the following:

> Only an idiot or a liar would attempt to deny what is patent to anyone. Skin color and hair type are only symbols of a constellation of genetic differences that are responsible for gross statistical variations in physical strength and agility, emotional and behavioral norms, and the various components of intelligence. Since this civilization and culture were created by ethnic groups from Northern Europe, it is inevitable that such groups will do well in a society that they are by nature adapted to live in.

That is why treatments of present immigration policies in the context of the policies of the last century are fundamentally dishonest. Immigrants of the 19th century, mostly from the various nations of Europe, successfully adapted to life in the United States, assimilated our British-derived culture, and made largely positive contributions to our country *because* they were Europeans and thus shared, for the most part, in the Greco-Roman-Christian heritage that underpins the culture of all European nations.

America's founders

Non-Europeans, coming to the U.S. for economic reasons and finding American society and culture very different from the society and culture of the lands of their birth, tend naturally to try to alter their adopted land so that it resembles more closely the country they abandoned. That peculiarity is a function of human nature: truly, "there is no place like home," and that is not theory, but an indisputable fact of life. Apprehending this tendency, Thomas Jefferson, writing in 1782, warned against the pitfalls inherent in irresponsible immigration policies and what is today called "multiculturalism":

> They [foreign immigrants] will bring with them the principles of the government they leave, imbibed in their early youth; or if able to throw them off, it will be in exchange for an unbounded licentiousness, passing as is usual, from one extreme to another. It would be a miracle were they to stop precisely at the point of temperate liberty. Their principles with their language, they will transmit to their children. In proportion to their numbers, they will share with us in the legislation. They will infuse into it their spirit, warp and bias its direction, and render it a heterogeneous, incoherent, distracted mass.

Alexander Hamilton, likewise, instructs Americans to heed reality and beware the hazards of massive immigration by peoples still devoted to their former homelands. He declares bluntly that "particular attachment to any foreign nation is an exotic sentiment which, where it exists, must derogate from the exclusive affection due to our own country." The best course, Hamilton notes, would be "to render the people of this country as homogeneous as possible" for that policy "must tend as much as any other circumstance to the permanency of their union and prosperity."

Elsewhere, Hamilton stresses his concerns for the future of the infant republic when he states: "The influx of foreigners must, therefore, tend to produce a heterogeneous compound; to change and corrupt the national spirit; to complicate and confound public opinion; to introduce foreign propensities. In the composition of society, the harmony of ingredients is all-important, and whatever tends to a discordant intermixture must have an injurious tendency."

In other words, the more culturally alike a populace is, the better the chance of making a success of a society and a nation. Washington, Franklin, Madison, Adams, Ames, and others spoke similarly. None was afflicted with that strange malady, so prevalent today, in which any culture on Earth—especially the most primitive—is valued more highly than our own. They proclaimed what must be seen as a solid consensus on the subject: immigration is a grave matter, requiring enormous vigilance and possessing a genuine potential for calamity.

The Founding Fathers are ignored today by Establishment circles and such views as those we have just considered are denounced as thoroughly "old fashioned," at best, and "racist," at worst. The assumption in contemporary academia and in the media seems to be that educated men today know more than educated men 200 years ago, and so, they reason, it is perfectly safe to ignore the counsel of the Founders in these matters. But the Founders knew more, not less, than most moderns. They were fully cognizant of the lessons of history, since most could, and did, read such histories in the original classical tongues. What is more important, our ancestors were honest men who spoke their minds. None was inclined to truckle before special interests or to cringe in the face of subversive ideologues brandishing inane verbal bludgeons.

During the so-called Age of Enlightenment, in the 18th century, secular philosophers developed a notion of human beings that was singularly shallow and unidimensional. Man, in the view of the Enlightenment theorists, was essentially a rational, economic entity. Opposing views were largely passed over, forgotten, or suppressed. The traditional view, for example, insists that humankind possesses a multiplicity of dimensions, that man is an enormously complex creature, that certain flaws in human nature are persistent, and that man's spiritual and cultural attributes are signal components in determining his economic and political life. All of this was derided as foolish, antediluvian superstition.

Furthermore, these radical theorists postulated, man is a wholly malleable creature, the perfect plastic material for experiments in social engineering. It was assumed that a "new man" might well be fabricated. The French Revolution, the Bolshevik Revolution, socialist movements, and the modern welfare state all find their source in those theories, and the colossal mounds of corpses produced by many of these experiments bear stark witness to the error, and ruthlessness, of that school of thought. The deliberate forcing together of peoples of unlike or rival cultures is also related to the same fanciful ideas, and generates the same tragic sequelae.

Human societies and cultures do not interact with one another in the ways the utopians maintain they do. Most of the world's societies are not tolerant, not charitable, not magnanimous, and not evenhanded towards the representatives of other societies and cultures. Events in history as well as in our own time serve equally to prove the point. Even at this very moment, as we read quietly in the comfort of our homes, human beings are ripping to pieces artificially contrived societies in which culturally disparate populations have been thrown together. The litany of human catastrophe is seemingly endless: the murderous conflicts that bedevil Rwanda, Nigeria, South Africa, the Indian subcontinent, and the Balkans are only the most recent illustrations of that phenomenon of hostile cultural groups giving vent to an impulse so trenchantly described by Dr. Samuel Francis as "secret compulsions to spill each other's blood." And so, human beings and human society are not nearly so ductile as Leftist theorists would have us believe.

How societies succeed

No scholar has ever developed a theory of human society that encompasses all aspects of life, though a few men have tried, and one or two have come close. Nonetheless, there exist sufficient data from historical and sociological evidence to enable us to reach certain definite conclusions. The conservative theologian, Harold O. J. Brown, in an essay on the writings of Henri Bergson published recently in *The Religion and Society Report*, discusses some of the prerequisites for a successfully functioning society.

> What instinct does for the bee society, a sense of obligation does for human society. Human beings are to a great extent free agents,

and when confronted with any task or assignment, have to make a decision of the will, a choice, to perform it—or, as the case frequently is, not to perform it. The majority of these decisions are made out of a sense of obligation, frequently without an explicit reason or justification: *Il faut parce qu'il faut*, "You must because you must," [Bergson's] English translator puts it. Every society has its language: many of the obligations that enable society to function are reflected in the words of the language its members use and may not be readily understood or mean the same thing if literally translated into another language. The vast network of obligations that make up society form a fabric. A certain number of individual threads can be broken or pulled out of the social fabric without destroying it, but there is a limit to the extent to which this can be done without causing the fabric to unravel. . . . Functioning societies are closed, sometimes in the narrow sense of a very small community that is isolated from all others, but even larger societies such as nations are closed in the sense that they have a unifying network of obligations, usually a common language and generally a religion, at least in some general sense of the word, all of which mark them off from other human societies. A universal human society is not possible, or not yet possible, because a society can exist only on the basis of shared obligations, and obligations cannot be shared, or can be shared only with difficulty, where there is no common language or culture.

But there is an exception to the rule and Dr. Brown gives, at this point, an example of the sort of artificially concocted society in which culturally diverse people can and do function together successfully, at least for a while—a unique military formation.

It is possible to create a kind of society without a common language, religion, and culture, if it can be closed in another way and if a means can be found to communicate a sense of obligation. The French Foreign Legion offers an example of such a society: it assembles men from different countries, languages, religions, social classes, and races, of varying social backgrounds, and molds them together into a highly cohesive, unique society. The Legion's Latin motto, *Legio patria nostra* (The Legion is our Fatherland), symbolizes this new reality. The sense of shared obligation is created by the imposition of a common language—the French—and very clearly by closing the society—placing its members in specific units, keeping them close together, and confining them to their training camp until the society is sufficiently well constituted to permit them to leave camp and circulate in the more open society of the surrounding civilian world.

Is it coincidental that Dr. Brown's example is a military organization that must be, by its very nature, highly authoritarian? Indeed, it is no coincidence. "Multiculturalism" actually works, wherever naked force is employed to make it work. Unquestionably, the foregoing furnishes the reason that the only relatively successful models in history for "multicultural" or "pluralistic" societies have been, by necessity, absolutist despotisms—the Roman Empire, the USSR, and Tito's Yugoslavia, to mention only three. These examples, if present trends continue, may be prototypes for our own future. Brown concludes:

. . . it is simply not possible to have a functioning society with the kind of pluralism and multiculturalism that [Ben] Wattenberg envisages in his argument for open immigration. Indeed, neither the words pluralism nor multiculturalism are adequate to describe the kind of confusion and disorder that would reign; we propose a new word, multipluralism: pluralism of values, pluralism of language, pluralism of education, pluralism of religion, pluralism of varieties of nonreligion, etc., etc., *ad nauseam*.

The lesson, which Dr. Brown draws from the writings of Bergson, is crystal clear. Despite the theses of utopian philosophers that human nature is infinitely changeable and that one may put together society in any shape or form one wishes, a more sober view is supported strongly by perceptive observers of society and history.

In a separate essay, Brown quotes another modern scholar, the late Bertrand de Jouvenel, as follows: "As people belong to the same culture by use of the same language, so they belong to the same society by the understanding of the same moral language. As this common moral language extends, so does society; as it breaks up, so does society." We see therefore that there can be no true society where people share nothing in common. However strict and edifying Islamic moral teaching may be in Saudi Arabia, however colorful Hindu ceremonies may be in India, however abstruse Buddhist philosophy may be in the Far East, and however passionate the devotees of Voodoo may be in Haiti or Brazil, none of these religious views are in harmony with Christianity, nor can they be harmonized with Christian moral teaching and with life in a country where laws and customs are supposed to be based on a Christian worldview.

The only relatively successful models in history for "multicultural" or "pluralistic" societies have been . . . absolutist despotisms.

Our American Founders were far from utopians. Their view of society was practical and down-to-earth. Though they fought a war for independence from Great Britain, known as the American Revolution, they did nothing to overturn established social and cultural patterns. Even the new government they devised, while unique in all the world, bears the conspicuous impress of its British antecedents. These men were above all else restrained, temperate, and conservative.

In contrast, and not at all surprisingly, Bill Clinton recently expressed the wish that, "somehow, between the government, the churches, and the schools, we could teach people not only to resolve their differences, but to understand that America has the opportunity to become the world's first truly multiethnic, rainbow society, where we can embrace their differences." It need not be pointed out that Mr. Clinton is hardly the appropriate person to be preaching moral ideals to anyone. Be that as it may, the Founding Fathers, without question, would have been appalled at the thought of a President of the United States indulging in such perilous, shallow pipe dreams.

In connection with the views of the American Founding Fathers, we have already mentioned the propensity of immigrants to try to change their new homeland so that it more closely simulates the lands from which they came. When America was still inwardly robust and when our belief in the superiority of our way of life was still undiluted, immigrants were not given the chance to do this. "Adapt or leave" was the operative attitude in those days. In these closing years of the 20th century we are not so fortunate.

The changing face of America

When we ponder the news items that follow, let us remember that while attempts at altering our society reflect in part on the immigrant "rights" groups involved, they are not solely culpable. The poltroonery of American politicians, and some American citizens, in grovelling before the unjustified demands of these representatives of alien cultures, and in initiating some of the outrages themselves, are also to blame and are indicative of the profound psychological illness that grips much of our nation today, corroborating vividly the clever adage that people who bite the hand that feeds them usually lick the boots that kick them.

- Immigrant "rights" groups in San Antonio, Texas have demanded that the site of the Alamo, long a symbol for Texans and Americans of courage in the face of adversity and love of freedom, be "renovated" so as no longer to be, as it is now in their opinion, "racist" and an insult to "Mexican-Americans." If such groups succeed the "new" Alamo will de-emphasize the 1836 Texas War for Independence and instead stress the Mexican and Indian cultures of the region. To underscore their displeasure with traditional interpretations of American history, some of the multiculturalists have dubbed the heroes of the Alamo "corrupt scoundrels and land-grabbers."

- A school district in New Jersey, in which recent immigrants from India have become a significant political force, voted to re-name one of the local schools in honor of Mohandas Gandhi, and voted tax money to erect a statue of the Indian social reformer at the school. Meanwhile, the City Council of San Jose, California has voted to spend $500,000 of the taxpayers' money to erect a statue honoring the ancient pagan Aztec god, Quetzacoatl. Sponsors of the project claim that the city must honor citizens of "Hispanic" heritage (we should remember, in this regard, that Quetzacoatl obviously has nothing whatever to do with genuine Hispanic, or Christian Spanish, culture).

- The Multicultural Education Committee of the Cambridge, Massachusetts public school system recently recommended that the school holiday calendar change the names of traditional holidays. The reasons given are that Americans must learn to be more "inclusive" of all cultural groups and not to "offend" new immigrants. Under the proposal, Columbus Day would become "Peoples of America Day," Christmas becomes "Winter Vacation," and St. Patrick' s Day "Evacuation Day" (apparently referring to the evacuation of Japanese during the opening stages of World War II). In Long Beach, California, it is proposed that Thanksgiving Day become "Diversity Day" since new Third World immigrants "cannot identify" with the arrival of Pilgrims from Europe. Donna Shalala, Bill Clinton's Secretary of Health and Human Services, has insisted that Thanksgiving Day be transformed into a "White American Day of Remorse," on which day Americans of European ancestry are supposed to flog themselves over the alleged theft of America from the Amerinds.

Plainly, if the multiculturalists among our recent immigrants, and among native-born Americans, have their way, not only will the face of America be changed beyond all possibility of recognition, the substance itself will be transformed. That which makes our country unique, which makes America what historically it is, and Americans historically what they are, will be gone forever.

America's enemies

In contrast to most patriotic, pro-American organizations, pro-immigration organizations, even pro-illegal immigration pressure groups, are both powerful and well financed. This raises perfectly legitimate questions as to who is financing the drive to convert America from a country peopled largely by Europeans to one more closely resembling the Third World.

Big American corporations, the same ones that gave their support to NAFTA [North American Free Trade Agreement], and tax-exempt, Leftist foundations are the chief culprits here. For example, between 1986 and 1992, the Ford Foundation gave a total of $7,300,000 to the pro-illegal immigration group, the Mexican American Legal Defense and Educational Fund (MALDEF). Among other things, MALDEF strenuously supports the "right" of illegal Mexican immigrants to vote in U.S. elections. That same foundation has also handsomely supported other radical groups, giving $3,000,000 during the same period to the National Council of La Raza ("La Raza" meaning "The Race," a reference to people of Mexican and Latin-American ancestry) and $600,000 to the League of United Latin American Citizens.

> *[There is a] drive to convert America from a country peopled largely by Europeans to one more closely resembling the Third World.*

The Eastern Establishment, multi-national corporations, and giant, tax-exempt foundations envision an America where people's lives are no longer animated by their traditions, where there is no genuine heritage worth fighting for, where "average Americans" are little more than a faceless, mindless, rootless *fellaheen*, and where an upright and alert citizenry has been supplanted by an effortlessly controlled, materialistically oriented herd of "consumers," driven this way or that by a captive media and by tawdry commercial interests. While all of this is true also of Leftist politicians, like President Clinton, it is doubly true of Establishment "conservatives." Those so-called conservatives who supported NAFTA are, in the main, the same men who consistently betray us on the question of immigration. As Samuel Francis wrote in 1991 during the Bush Administration,

> The megastate and its masters can play with bombs in Bagdad and Bosnia all they want, save as many Somalians as can be rounded up, and count as many beans as they can find, but those enterprises will not preserve a civilization or a nation whose founding demographic core is facing a slow extinction and whose leaders have forgotten what civilization means and have come to regard their own nation as a barrier to be broken down and discarded.

Dr. Francis has further observed that, according to our own Census Bureau, in roughly a half-century, people of European ancestry will no longer constitute a majority in the United States of America. "By that time," he says, "the change will certainly have been completed so far as the old American civilization is concerned, but we probably will not have to wait that long to witness it."

The economist and sociologist, Vilfredo Pareto, comments in one of his many works that if a people should allow itself to become effete, cowardly, and too comfortable—that is, should they allow the vigor that previously distinguished them to disappear—then such people are bound to be swept away by revolution, displacement by outsiders, or some other radical social change. "It is amazing to see," Pareto writes, "how in imperial Rome the members of the elite committed suicide or allowed themselves to be assassinated without the slightest defense, as long as it pleased Caesar. We are equally amazed when we see the nobles of France die on the Guillotine, instead of going down fighting." Had they resisted, he writes, they might have prevailed and not perished.

Will someone, centuries from now, write similarly of the descendants of those liberty-loving men who colonized this land almost 500 years ago, who built a great nation, and who gave it the finest government known to history? Let us spare no effort to ensure that we are not so judged, that the America that we love does not perish, and that our civilization and way of life are preserved and strengthened.

4

The White Race
Must Be Saved

David Lane

David Lane is an inmate serving a forty-year sentence for murder, rack-eteering, and robbery at the federal penitentiary in Florence, Colorado.

The White race must grasp the reality that it faces imminent ex-tinction. The facts are these: the White race cannot survive with-out countries exclusively its own; it cannot share Gods or religion with another race. Religious and government institutions are try-ing to destroy the White race with poisonous lies. The race can be saved only if it listens to, believes in, and disseminates this mes-sage: We must secure the existence of our people and a future for White children.

I consider this to be one of the most important articles I've ever written because it deals with the solution. So I hope readers will give it serious consideration. If, yes if, we focus our efforts on exposing the situation as it actually is, we can win.

By 1995 it is possible to educate tens of millions of White people to the reality that their race faces imminent extinction, and why that would be the greatest tragedy in all eternity. After that is done, victory is in-evitable. Victory meaning a secure and exclusively White country, or countries, for the preservation and advancement of the White Aryan race. Such a victory is our goal.

To achieve a great and difficult goal requires several things. First we must identify, name and hallow the goal. Second we must resolve to achieve that goal, no matter what the cost. In this case that implies dis-ciplined fanaticism, meaning total commitment, combined with reason and judgement. Thirdly, we must have a plan of action. This plan of ac-tion must take into account the successes and failures of the past, and the tactics of the enemy.

For decades I've watched individuals and splintered factions, ostensi-bly dedicated to White racial survival, as they rise, fall, quibble, and ulti-mately self destruct. And for years, at least ever since creating the *Death of the White Race* pamphlet, I've attempted to show by hint and example,

David Lane, "Countdown to 1995," *WAR: White Aryan Resistance*, vol. 12, no. 1 (February 1993). Reprinted with permission.

the nature of successful racial literature. But still our people continue to play the enemies [sic] game by being diverted to irrelevant issues.

The problem for whites

So one more time let us define the problem and then we can outline a plan of action that will succeed.

The facts are these. Our race cannot survive without countries exclusively our own in which to propagate, protect, and promote our own kind. The inevitable result of racial integration is a percent of racial interbreeding every year. Over time that is racial death. Forced racial integration is therefore deliberate malicious genocide, the extermination of our specie. We are a small minority already, on earth.

America and the occupation governments of the once White countries deny us not only exclusively White countries, but White schools, White neighborhoods, White organizations, and everything necessary for our continued survival as a biological and cultural entity.

Now one more time on religion. We cannot share Gods, religion, holy books, with another race. Just as you cannot countries, flags, music, culture, sports, education, technology, women, territory, or anything else with another race. It destroys the sense of exclusivity, uniqueness, and value, necessary to racial survival. If you teach your children that the God of your race loves every fellow, black, brown, red, or yellow, then expect your daughter to love and produce some more rainbow creatures. If a negro fights in an army of "your" country then expect him in your schools, clubs, jobs, and bedrooms. The dominate [sic] religion of the once White countries, in almost all of its various cults and divisions is determinedly pushing race-mixing and their so-called brotherhood of universal man. You cannot take back a religion, if indeed it was ever ours, from a billion non-whites and brain dead race traitors.

Our race cannot survive without countries exclusively our own in which to propagate, protect, and promote our own kind.

We must recognize that the existing religious and governmental institutions are totally in the control of our racial enemies and are being used to destroy us. We cannot begin to refute the poison the enemy spreads through his control of all organs of information distribution. In churches, schools, talk shows, T.V., and everywhere we look we see our folk being mislead [sic] and channeled into pursuing other issues than our racial survival. The issue is not Jesus, Odin, negroes, jews, the alleged holocaust, Indians, a failed constitution, money, or material goods. The issues are, "Will the beauty of the White Aryan woman continue to exist on this earth, will White children have a future, and will our kind of civilization continue in centuries to come." If we are to succeed we must take these issues, which I sometimes call the 14 Words [see end of viewpoint], and beat them to death.

We must also understand the psychological impact of the siege mentality. The jews conquered the world with bogus tales of atrocities against their tribe. It has been one of their greatest unifying forces. We on the other hand are very real targets of the ultimate atrocity, the extermination of our specie.

We cannot even hope to debate the hundreds of misleading enemy scenarios. But if we all, in a concerted, unrelenting, and focused effort, work to drill into the minds of the masses, and to drive through the media curtain, one simple issue, we can succeed. As stated in [Lane's] *88 Precepts*, propaganda is a legitimate and necessary function in any struggle, and the elements of successful propaganda are S.E.R.B., simplicity, emotion, repetition, and brevity. During those brief moments when we are able to penetrate the media curtain, our message must be exactly to the point. The *88 Precepts* are designed to give short concise precise answers to friends and enemies alike. Also to make use of the focusing principles of numbering the laws. This was a highly successful technique devised for the Christian bible and there is nothing wrong with learning from the procedures used by others.

Our message

Our methods are dictated by historical experience, present circumstance, human psychology, and necessity. If we are to achieve our goal by 1995 we must focus on one thing. We must mount a fanatically determined effort to disseminate our message. That message was stated earlier in this article and will be repeated again shortly. It must be repeated over and over and over. Even if you are sick and tired of repeating it or hearing it. A wise man once counseled that when giving a speech containing an important message the speaker should first tell the audience what he was about to say, then say it, then tell them what he just said.

Call the radio talk shows every chance you get. But only state our message, and then get off the phone. Don't debate.

Install message center phones. This is vital, and if you can possibly do so you must. But every recording must begin with a repetition of our message, and end with the 14 words.

Write letters to the editor, but begin every letter with our message.

Produce publications, but every article must contain our message.

Produce *Race and Reason* type [television] shows, but every show must contain our message.

Produce leaflets and pamphlets, but every single one must contain our message.

Appear on the enemy media, but refuse to discuss anything except our message.

We . . . are very real targets of the ultimate atrocity, the extermination of our specie.

Grant an interview to an enemy reporter. Then make a short statement. Our message. End of interview. Period. We do not debate with swine.

If they try to draw you into discussion of their issues, tell them that under nature's laws, the motivations, history, affairs, and circumstances of other races, religions, or power systems, are not your concern. You obey the first law of nature, "The preservation of your own kind."

In summation; we can win, if we focus all our efforts on what is the only real issue. That is racial survival. We must break the media curtain and give our Folk the MESSAGE. In case you have already forgotten, here is the message again. Let us repeat it a hundred million times.

The message: Our race cannot survive without countries exclusively our own, in which to propagate, protect, and promote, our own kind. The inevitable result of racial integration is a percent of racial inter-breeding every year. Over time that is racial death. Forced racial integration is therefore deliberate malicious genocide, the extermination of our specie. We are a small minority on earth already.

America and the occupation governments of the once White countries deny us not only exclusively White countries, but also, White schools, White neighborhoods, White organizations, and everything necessary for our continued survival as a biological and cultural entity.

One more time on religion: We cannot share Gods, religion, holy books, with another race. Just as we cannot share countries, flags, music, culture, sports, education, technology, women, territory, or anything else, with another race. It destroys the senses of exclusivity, uniqueness and value necessary to racial survival. If you teach your children that the God of your race, "Loves every fellow, black, brown or yellow," then expect your daughter to love and produce some more such fellows. If a negro fights in an army of "YOUR" country (ha) then expect him in your schools, clubs, jobs, and bedrooms. The dominate [sic] religion in the once White countries, in almost all of it's [sic] various cults and divisions is determinedly pushing race-mixing and their brotherhood of universal mankind. You cannot take back a religion, if indeed it was ever ours, from a billion non-whites.

If the beauty of White Aryan women is to continue on earth, and if White children are to have a future, then our race must collectively resolve to obey nature's highest law, which is the preservation of one's own kind. There exists only one issue for any sane White person at this juncture in history. It can be summed up in just 14 words, which are, *"We must secure the existence of our people and a future for White children."* That is the message.

5

Blacks Should Embrace Black Nationalism

Askia Muhammad

Askia Muhammad hosts a weekly music show for radio station WPFW-FM in Washington, D.C.

Most blacks want the good life that America has to offer. But many blacks also embrace the message of the black Muslim organization Nation of Islam, whose founder Elijah Muhammad and present leader Louis Farrakhan condemn white America for its exploitation of blacks. The appeal of the Nation of Islam is its desire for discipline and its championing of black nationalism. Blacks should not try to be multicultural, which seems to mean denying their blackness in favor of being "people of color." Instead, blacks should know and be their black selves. Black nationalism—Nation-of-Islam style—is embedded into the core of black consciousness and culture.

"Did you hear about those church people killed by that tornado?" an old man asked me in an elevator in April 1994. "Yes. It's too bad," I replied, recalling the Palm Sunday tragedy that left 20 worshipers dead in their pews at Goshen United Methodist Church in Piedmont, Ala., while they listened to a hymn.

"Did you notice that all the people killed were white?" the black man said. I raised an eyebrow. The door opened as we reached his floor. "It's payback. That's what it is. It's payback for what they've done to us," he said before heading down the hall.

For a moment, like my interlocutor—and I dare say many other black Americans—I entertained the thought (however crass and uncivil it may seem) that God might have been expressing, or might one day yet to come express, vengeance which is His and presumably His alone to express, against white Americans.

It is here where America's racial divide becomes a gulf. Whites in this country by and large believe the United States to be a blessed nation that enjoys God's abundant grace. Blacks in surprising numbers are secretly praying for whites to be paid back for the injustices done to them during slavery and for their murdering the Indians, among other assorted crimes

Askia Muhammad, "What's Right with the Nation of Islam," *The Washington Post National Weekly Edition*, June 6-12, 1994. Reprinted by permission of the author.

and misdemeanors.

If viewed in this context, it is easier to understand how a message like Louis Farrakhan's and Elijah Muhammad's before him—a message that condemns white America for its wars and sins and economic exploitation of darker peoples around the globe—can resonate among black people, who have otherwise been so patriotic and trusting of the promise of a better life one day in America. But blacks are not born wishing for the fall of America. Most want the good life the country has to offer. Most earnestly seek that "dream" all their lives.

Pursuing the dream

I did. When I was 19 in 1964, I was a member of the U.S. Naval Reserve. I was a college student who drove a red British roadster. I thought I was on my way to an interesting tour of duty as a naval officer after I completed my schoolwork and the officer candidate school [OCS] at Newport, R.I. Racial prejudice had revealed itself to me in my life in Southern California, but I shrugged it off.

I was a journalism major at Los Angeles City College in those days. Despite my many opinions about the burning racial issues of the mid-1960s, whenever I saw bow-tie wearing black men selling that newspaper, *Muhammad Speaks*, I would cross to the other side of the street, to avoid having to read what I thought was narrow propaganda that lacked journalistic credibility.

But then the riots started. Every summer there would be those race riots. Harlem in 1964. Watts in 1965. At Newport in the summer of 1967, I was ashamed for the first time to wear my Navy midshipman's uniform. There were riots 10 miles away in Providence. Hurley's Bar, which I had frequented in the black community, was under curfew, and the eight other blacks and myself (out of 2,500 total) at the Navy OCS were all slightly confused.

Then Martin Luther King was killed in 1968. I was a student at San Jose State at that time and I was outraged. I resigned from OCS for reasons of conscience. I had never been to a Nation of Islam meeting, though I had heard a speaker on campus in Los Angeles, and had fallen asleep once listening to Elijah Muhammad's weekly radio broadcast. I continued to pursue my conventional American dreams, with Stokely Carmichael and the Rev. Jesse Jackson emerging as the leaders I admired most.

I came to believe that there is no shame in what is known as black nationalist thinking.

Journalism now had even more promise for me. For two years I worked in the press room of the *Milpitas Post* and *East San Jose Sun* newspapers. In 1968, I was one of 12 blacks chosen to be an intern at *Newsweek* magazine. I met Bill Cosby. Vice presidents of companies like TRW and Northrop returned my calls. I was somebody.

But there was another appeal pulling on me. I wanted to be a part of the uplifting of my people. I had resolved after my *Newsweek* experience that I wanted to have a measurable impact on the lives of black people, not as a faceless slug of type that read "Charles K. Moreland Jr.," a name indistinguishable from the names of the white writers listed also in the magazine.

All over the country, the direction of the civil rights movement was being debated; disputes about the benefits of integration and/or coalitions between blacks and liberal whites, as compared to self-determination, grew hot. Two things became clear to me: Those who knew more, who seemed to be the most intelligent, the most articulate, seemed to carry the day in many arguments. And those who had discipline seemed able to get things done, seemed less at the mercy of white intervention.

Above all, I wanted to *know*. I wanted a command of black history. As I read Herbert Aptheker and W.E.B. DuBois and Richard Wright, I got angry about the conditions they wrote about. I discovered 19th century activists, including David Walker, Denmark Vesey, Nat Turner and Martin Delany, and intellectuals such as Frantz Fanon and Harold Cruse in this century. I saw that these thinkers had spawned younger contemporaries such as Frances Cress Welsing and Chancellor Williams. I felt that all of these talked, prophesied or performed a work themselves like that of Marcus Mosiah Garvey. And I came to believe that there is no shame in what is known as black nationalist thinking.

Why can't we try to know our black selves, try to be our black selves?

What tipped the scales in favor of the Nation of Islam for me was the desire for discipline, and my perception that not only did I personally need discipline but that everyone everywhere in my community also needed it. When I started attending meetings of the Nation of Islam in search of that discipline, I learned that the Nation was already a viable part of the black community.

I threw myself into the movement with the zeal of a new convert. I now proudly sold the newspaper I used to cross the street to avoid reading. I proselytized. I sold so many chicken dinners one weekend that I won a contest; first prize was an official Fruit of Islam uniform. I worked on the mosque public relations committee. I became the West Coast stringer for *Muhammad Speaks*.

In 1972, when there was an internal shakeup at *Muhammad Speaks*, I was picked by Muhammad himself to come to Chicago to work in the editorial office of his newspaper and printing plant. He told me to "see what is good and what is bad, and look out for the interests of the Nation." At first I was the copy editor; within a year I was the editor of the whole paper. I was the first registered Muslim to hold the job.

For two and a half years, I edited the paper, watching its circulation grow to 900,000 copies per week. Early in 1973, Muhammad instructed me to stop allowing writers to use the expression "blue-eyed devil" or any other offensive language in the newspaper referring to whites. At first, I was able to hold the line against zealous adherents with axes to grind. But when a black reporter from the *New York Times* reported in December 1973 that Muhammad was deathly ill and that his movement was plagued by dissension, the dike burst. Muslims began attacking whites wholesale in print again and accusing the black reporter of doing the bidding of the white man.

After two weeks, Muhammad ordered a halt to the hostilities. We were sitting at his dinner table. One of his ministers was reading another attack article out loud for approval for publication. "No!" Muhammad said emphatically, midway through the reading. "I'm tired of this. It sounds like a pack of big black dogs barking, 'Woof, woof, woof.' And then when you look to see what all the noise is about there is this little white one over there going 'Yip, yip, yip.'" We never published another racial slur in *Muhammad Speaks*.

In early 1975, Muhammad reportedly died (although believers like myself maintain that he is still alive). His sons, Warith Deen and Jabril, forced me out as they took over the leadership of the Nation, changing its philosophy and changing the name of the newspaper to the *Balalian News*. In 1978, Louis Farrakhan, who was Muhammad's national representative, reestablished the movement based on Elijah Muhammad's teachings. By then I had moved on to work for the *Chicago Daily Defender*, and then into radio journalism.

Today, when I look back on my time with the Nation, I'm embarrassed that I ever doubted what I now believe to be the truth about Muhammad's teachings. I know I have paid a price professionally for that belief. I maintain that Muhammad was right in the things that he taught, and I see confirmation of his message even by white authorities all the time. For example, *Newsweek* and *Science* magazines published similar cover stories a few years back declaring that the "biological Eve"—the first female homo sapiens—was an African. Muhammad said basically the same thing when he began his mission in the 1930s—that blacks were the first people on Earth, that the black woman is the "Mother of Civilization."

Controversial messages

Still black nationalism in general and Muhammad's message in particular are verboten in so-called enlightened circles. Blacks who are otherwise liberal or even radical on most issues often prefer to distance themselves from the Nation of Islam and Farrakhan. Some of the reasons are religious. It is no easier for Christians, black or white, to accept the "new revelation" from God, called Islam, than it is for Jews to embrace the idea of Jesus. On top of that, Muhammad's message is a dramatic departure from traditional Islam because of his insistence that Allah appeared in person in the United States in 1930, teaching the new Islamic dogma which says that God is a member of the Original Black Nation, and that whites are inherently evil. It is a kind of "chosen people" argument—that the whole world is waiting for black Americans to achieve their full potential and lead the world to peace and progress. So it comes as no surprise that white Americans are quick to declare that anyone who does not join in the ritual denunciations of Farrakhan is persona non grata.

Never mind that Americans recognize the tragic but legitimate differences between "Green" and "Orange" Caucasians in Northern Ireland and between the Bosnian and Serbian and Croatian Caucasians in the former Yugoslavia. In reaction to the obvious unfairness of American "Jim Crow" laws, America has succumbed to what I think of as "melting pot madness," requiring that blacks must try to be "multicultural." For whites this may mean accommodating other races and groups, but for blacks it seems to mean denying our blackness in favor of being "people of color" or "Third World" people. Why can't we try to know our black selves, try to be our black selves?

So today, as I continue to struggle to raise my voice concerning the good work that the Nation accomplishes in the tradition of self-help and black pride that Muhammad espoused, I am surprised that so many whites especially see the message of self-love I embrace as being hateful. Yes, we are wary and mistrustful of whites and want to keep our relationship at arm's length but we don't hate white people just because they are white—any more than we hate lions because they roar. We just don't want to be lion food. The social reality I know is that Muhammad's message reforms, not just the down-and-out blacks who are touched while they're in jail, on welfare, on drugs, but black people in all walks of life who are in need of a positive message of spiritual uplift.

That's where I disagree with Khalid Abdul Muhammad, who was shot in 1994 after a speech at the University of California at Riverside. Though I've known him for more than a dozen years to be an astute and intrepid man, his provocative remarks are making it impossible for Farrakhan or other members of the Nation be taken seriously outside the circle of those who are the most radical to begin with. Instead of leading marches of other fearless black men in neighborhoods where drugs and violence have made prisoners of our old, our women and our children, he and his young supporters are leading derisive chants that exaggerate the already strident message taught by his mentors.

Elijah Muhammad's teaching, it should be remembered, has always been a literal message, intended to be, in his words, "right and exact." His first lesson for converts was to copy a letter, line for line, word for word, in blue or black ink (not pencil), dotting every "i" and crossing every "t" before they would be accepted for membership. Those who could not read or write learned how. Smudges and erasures were not accepted. Nowhere in the 40-page official liturgy that followed that enrollment is there any specific reference to Jews, or to the pope, or to South African whites, or to any of Khalid Muhammad's other recent targets.

Now thanks to Khalid Muhammad's rhetorical excesses, instead of delivering the comfort and peace that trained Nation of Islam security guards have shown they can deliver to residents of out-of-control housing projects, the Nation is answering charges of antisemitism and race hate. Now there is a proposed amendment to the Department of Housing and Urban Development appropriation bill that could make it impossible for Nation of Islam firms to win government contracts. Now, because of Khalid Muhammad's speeches at Howard University, students there are reporting difficulties finding jobs and summer internships.

This is too high a price to pay, just because Elijah Muhammad once taught something similar (and he distanced himself from it later in life) or because some people today get a thrill out of hearing it. Farrakhan's dilemma, and why he can't denounce Khalid Muhammad outright, arises from the fact that those rantings always contain a kernel of the original teachings. For Farrakhan to condemn Khalid Muhammad would be to appear to change Elijah Muhammad's message, of which he is only the custodian.

New voices

Since my conversion to Islam in 1969, I have spoken with white people to whom I had once been especially close and I told them what I would tell any white person: I know it's difficult, but try to understand, black people are speaking with new voices today—often angry voices, militant voices, uncompromising voices, shrill voices, voices that sometimes seem to scapegoat and over-generalize.

Please wait and watch Farrakhan in the fullness of time, not just in the passion of the moment. Understand that his roots and his sacrifices for the upliftment of blacks are deep, and that he enjoys the confidence and full trust of ordinary, thoughtful people like me, who come by our embrace of black nationalism through the same kind of arduous channels that any person comes by any other philosophy.

It's too late to put Farrakhan, or the genie of separate destinies for America's black and white nations, back into the bottle. Black nationalism—Nation-of-Islam style—is embedded into the core of black consciousness and our culture. From pork-free diets and bean pies to red bow ties, like it or not, increasing numbers of blacks have chosen to listen to and be guided by their own notions of right and wrong and those notions are clearly influenced by perception of race.

Witness a recent poll of blacks conducted by the University of Chicago: Sixty-eight percent of those surveyed said black people should control the government in predominantly black communities; 74 percent said blacks should control the economies in those areas; 77 percent said American society is not fair to blacks. In fact, the inevitable conflict between black nationalism and conventional American norms is, as DuBois wrote in "The Souls of Black Folks," fought out in almost every black person, "two souls, two thoughts, two unreconciled strivings, two warring ideals in one dark body."

6

Demanding a Multicultural Curriculum

June Jordan

June Jordan is a poet and a professor of African-American and women's studies at the University of California at Berkeley. She is a regular columnist for the Progressive, *a monthly liberal magazine.*

The time has come for America to abandon its traditional, white-male bias in education. Minorities limited to only the study of the white Western canon threaten to become estranged from their heritage and unaware of their loss. A glaring example of America's biased and distorted education—and its racist undertones—is the teaching of the bombing of Pearl Harbor. The teaching of this event and America's war against Japan remains a repugnant attack on the people of Japan and Japanese-Americans. Growth in minority populations demands that students be given a multicultural curriculum to learn from the perspectives of more minority cultures.

Thirty years ago, white publications loved to headline stories about my neighborhood, my family, and me, with three words: "The Negro Problem."

I remember rapid adjustment of my mind from a state of plain puzzlement to anger. I'd be passing by a subway newsstand and there I'd see it, that incendiary formulation that implied that we, "Negroes," had created our own difficulties and, further, that we, "Negroes," were the only ones who could, or should, give a damn. So many Americans succumbed to that game!

Again and again, slick magazines and daily papers blamed the victim and erased, or exculpated, the perpetrators of the crime. This was all the more remarkable as the context was one of wild white violence, which meant that Negro "difficulties" might well include catching a bullet in the brain if your local sheriff discovered you trying to register to vote.

What finally blew away these print-media fabrications—what finally replaced them with factual knowledge leading to a national and world-wide uproar that, in turn, led to the Civil Rights Act of 1960 and other pivotal laws—was the camera: Regardless of the caption beneath the pho-

June Jordan, "Toward a Manifest New Destiny," *The Progressive*, February 1992. Reprinted by permission from *The Progressive*, 409 E. Main St., Madison, WI 53703.

tograph, regardless of the text read by the (white) voice-over on film, visual reports of our history carried the day. You could not watch a white man screaming as he overturned, set afire, and burned up a Greyhound bus and then still be confused about who, exactly, had done what, where, and when.

I wonder what it will take to blow away an equally fictitious, an equally venomous print-media construction of our time: the so-called Politically Correct or PC Controversy.

I would like to assume that an eyeball basis for analysis and opinion could decide things. And perhaps, at the last, that will happen. But I cannot forget going on a lunch date, once, with Victor Navasky, editor of *The Nation*.

We met at his office above the congestion of 14th Street in Manhattan. As we walked to the restaurant of his choice, a few blocks away, we moved among and around crowds of black and Puerto Rican as well as white New Yorkers. I was asking Victor how come *The Nation* had never hired a single black columnist. He seemed exasperated by my inquiry. He could not comprehend how anything calling itself *The Nation* but staffed entirely by white men could seem peculiar, if not offensive, to anyone. He could not imagine that an American who was different from himself in serious, immutable ways—he could not imagine that such an American writer might bring to *The Nation* something important: information and perspectives that he and his white associates could not otherwise encounter or possess.

"Are you saying," he asked in an avuncular tone, "are you implying that there is A Black Point of View?"

I answered him—"Yes"—and I attempted to explain that there is an absolute difference between his white male history and my own. I argued that such a chasmic separation in experience must produce significant divergences of viewpoint, expectations, and the like.

But Victor was not interested. Comfortably seated at his regular table inside his restaurant of choice, he knew something I was only beginning to understand: There is difference, and there is power. And who holds the power shall decide the meaning of difference. Victor held the power, and he had decided that ideas and opinions and feelings that belong to anybody markedly different from himself are ideas and convictions that do not count.

Victor embodies a one-man definition—a big part, the American media part—of the problem of knowledge in the United States. Too much of what we know or don't know depends upon unaccountable individual values and the sometimes whimsical happenstance of one man's or one powerful family's or one corporate CEO's political biography. In the case of Navasky, here was a white man blind and deaf except to a mirror universe of his kin and kind. And what could I do about it?

America's many peoples

I have worked here, inside this country, and I have kept my eyes open, everlastingly. What I see today does not support a media-concocted controversy where my life or the lives of African-Americans, Native-Americans, Chicano-Americans, Latin-Americans, and Asian-Americans amount to arguable fringe or freak components of some theoretical netherland. We have become the many peoples of this nation—nothing less than that. I do not accept that we, American peoples of color, signify anything optional or dubious or marginal or exotic or anything in any way less valuable, less necessary, less sacred than white America.

I do not perceive current issues of public education as issues of politically correct or incorrect curriculum. In a straight line back to James Baldwin who, twenty-eight years ago, begged us, blackfolks, to rescue ourselves by wrestling white people out of the madness of their megalomania and delusion, I see every root argument about public education turning upon definitions of sanity and insanity. Shall we submit to ceaseless lies, fantastic misinformation, and fantastic omissions? Shall we agree to the erasure of our beleaguered, heterogeneous truth? Shall we embrace traditions of insanity and lose ourselves and the whole real world?

Or shall we become "politically correct" as fast as we can and defend and engage the multifoliate, overwhelming, and ultimately inescapable actual life that our myriad and disparate histories imply?

In America, in a democracy, who shall the people know if not our many selves? What shall we aim to learn about the universe if not the entire, complicated truth of it, to the best of our always limited abilities? What does public education in a democratic state require if not the rational enlightenment of as many of the people as possible? But how can you claim to enlighten a child and then tell him that the language of his mother is illegal?

Barco de Refugiados
by Lorna Dee Cervantes

Mamá me crío sin lenguaje.
Soy huérfano de mi nombre español.
Las palabras son extrañas,
tartamudeando en mi lengua.
Mis ojos ven el espejo, mi reflejo:
piel de bronce, cabello negro.

Siento que soy un cautivo
a bordo de un barco de refugiados.
El barco que nunca atraca.
El barco que nunca atraca.

Refugee Ship

Mama raised me without language.
I'm orphaned from my Spanish name.
The words are foreign, stumbling
on my tongue. I see in the mirror
my reflection: bronzed skin, black hair.

I feel I am a captive
aboard the refugee ship.
The ship that will never dock.
El barco que nunca atraca.

(Reprinted by permission of Lorna Dee Cervantes.)

White warriors for the preservation of the past and for a mythical status quo, white warriors for the insane, invoke supposedly scary scenarios in which Platonic Dialogues disappear from the core of academic studies and students instead examine the teachings of Buddha or the political writings of Frederick Douglass. I look at these mainly conjectural outbursts and I say to myself, "What's all the fuss about?"

The favorite, last-resort accusation of these white warriors for the insane, for the traditional white-male-dominated canon of required readings in American higher education, is this: That the barbarian leadership of us, the barbarian hordes, basically aims to subvert and challenge and eliminate the intellectual icons of Western civilization. Commonly, this accusation produces a good deal of apologetic shuffling on the part of the alleged barbarians, the so-called Politically Correct. Well, I am one barbarian who will not apologize. You bet that's one of my basic aims! Why would anyone suppose that I or any Native-American or any Asian-American would willingly worship at the altar of traditional white Western iconography?

> The white man killed my father
> Because my father was proud
> The white man raped my mother
> Because my mother was beautiful
> The white man wore out my brother in the hot sun
> of the roads
> Because my brother was strong
> Then the white man came to me
> His hands red with blood
> Spat his contempt into my black face
> Out of his tyrant's voice:
> "Hey boy, a basin, a towel, water."
>   *—David Diop, "Le temps du martyre."*

> As the contradiction among the features
> creates the harmony of the face
> we proclaim the oneness of the suffering
> and the revolt
> of all the peoples on all the face of the earth
> and we mix the mortar of the age of brotherhood
> out of the dust of idols.
>   *—Jacques Roumain, "Bois-D'Ebene."*

(The Diop and Roumain verses are reprinted from Frantz Fanon's *Black Skin, White Masks*, by permission of Grove Press.)

The gods of the white Western world from Jahweh ("Vengeance is mine, saith the Lord") to Jesus ("Blessed are the meek") to Dante to Nietzsche to Milton to T.S. Eliot to Wallace Stevens: What have they done for me? Show me one life saved by any of these gods! Show me one colored life!

As you descend deeper and deeper into media hysteria about alleged or impending "violations of the canon" and "rape of the foundations of Western civilization," the smell of brain rot and unmitigated white supremacist ideology becomes unmistakable.

Suppose, for example, suppose I skipped English literature and Shakespeare altogether and instead I studied Chinese: Chinese history and Chinese literature. A quarter of the human beings on the planet are Chinese. And I know next to nothing about them. I do not really understand why my friend who was born in the Year of the Dragon cannot marry her beloved who was born in the Year of the Dog. But I can recite to you a score of beautiful lines from Elizabethan sonnets. And I do not altogether fault what I know, but I do not view my ignorance as acceptable. And if I had to choose between those sonnets and Chinese history, and if I chose Chinese history, who could criticize me, and on what grounds?

It depends, of course, on the purpose of education. Uncontested, until now, the purpose of American schooling has been to maintain the powerful in power. And so, traditional materials for the American classroom have presented every war, every battle, every dispute, every icon of knowledge required by "higher" education in the image of the powerful so as to serve the interests of the powerful who need the rest of us to believe they are really nice guys who take off their boots before they take over your house and your land.

Reinforcing the skewed effects of traditional materials is the homogeneous identity of teachers and faculty who persist, increasingly out of sync, with the heterogeneous student bodies whose intellectual development they must oversee. For example, in California public schools, teachers remain 82 per cent white while so-called minority students occupy 54 per cent of classroom seats. Such a dramatic disjuncture does not bode well for imperative curricular change that will serve the cultural and historical needs of these new (young) Americans.

Supreme Court Justice Clarence Thomas—whose four law clerks are, every one of them, white men, and whose accomplishments as former head of the Equal Employment Opportunity Commission do not cleanly distinguish him from David Duke—wonderfully illustrates the results of traditional "higher" American education. So do those Japanese-Americans who cannot proclaim, too fervently or too frequently, how lamentable was the Japanese bombing of Pearl Harbor.

If you're not white, if you're not an American white man, and you travel through the traditional twistings and distortions of the white Western canon, you stand an excellent chance of ending up *nuts*: Estranged if not opposed to yourself and your heritage and, furthermore, probably unaware of your estrangement, your well-educated self-hatred.

Pearl Harbor

The last seven days leading to the fiftieth anniversary of Pearl Harbor were particularly difficult. At moments, I felt overwhelmed as the coast-to-coast unanimity of know-nothing, racist blatherings about December 7, 1941, grew louder and ever more obviously self-righteous and unbalanced by even a respectable modicum of trustworthy scholarship or unbiased inquiry into the Japanese side of the story.

Of course, any concern to secure the Japanese side of the story would represent a concern that is Politically Correct. It would mean supposing that the Japanese people are not some subspecies of the human race, alias homo Americo, or whatever. It would mean supposing that the Japanese government did not lapse into a psychotic military fit that fateful morning but that, in fact, the Japanese government had its reasons for attacking that rather far-flung U.S. naval base, Pearl Harbor.

And I was nauseated by the unmitigated, ignorant, hate-mongering sanctimony of American leaders those past seven days. Is there, after all, another country as militaristic, as predatory, as imperial, as deadly as our own? Does the average American even have the glimmer of an adequate, sane education to respond to that question?

The lunacy of racist America, the insanity of Politically Incorrect education in racist America means that it's okay to advertise the atomic bombing of Hiroshima as "revenge" for the Japanese bombing of Pearl Harbor.

Asian peoples are the largest group of human beings on the planet.

This kind of pathological, complacent Asian-bashing is truly not all right: not morally or intellectually or, in any wise, defensible, sane behavior. And when I must wallow in this display of America's latest racist target—a target jeopardizing most of the human beings on the planet—then, yes, I get pretty damned upset. Here is a quote from the front page of *USA Today*, December 6, 1991:

"By 1941, Japan's campaign of Asian conquest was ten years old. Over Western protests the Japanese war machine had occupied Manchuria and invaded China. After the occupation of French Indochina the United States, Britain, and the Netherlands imposed a trade embargo, cutting Japan's oil supplies by 90 per cent. Japan quickly turned its attention to expropriating oil fields in the Dutch East Indies. To prevent U.S. interference, Tokyo mounted a bold plan to wipe out the U.S. fleet at Pearl Harbor, Hawaii, on December 7, 1941."

Okay. "By 1941, Japan's campaign of Asian conquest was ten years old." By 1941, how old was America's and England's and the Netherlands' campaign of Asian conquest? And what in the hell are you talking about when you say "French Indochina" and the "Dutch East Indies"?

Here is a poem that no English major in the U.S.A. will ever be required to read: It was written by the Japanese-Canadian poet and novelist Joy Kogawas, and it's entitled "Hiroshima Exit."

> In round round rooms of our wanderings
> Victims and victimizers in circular flight
> Fast pursuing fast
> Warning leaflets still drip down
> On soil heavy with flames,
> Black rain, footsteps, witnessings—
>
> The Atomic Bomb Memorial Building:
> A curiosity shop filled with
> Remnants of clothing, radiation sickness,
> Fleshless faces, tourists muttering
> "Well, they started it."
> Words jingle down
> "They didn't think about us in Pearl Harbor."
> They? Us?
> I tiptoe around the curiosity shop
> Seeking my target
> Precision becomes essential
> Quick. Quick. Before he's out of range.
> Spell the name
> American?
> Hiroshima?
>
> Air raid warnings wail bleakly
> Hiroshima
> Morning.
> I step outside
> And close softly the door
> Believing, believing
> That outside this store
> Is another door
>
> (Reprinted, with the permission of Greenfield Review Press, from
> *Breaking Silence: An Anthology of Contemporary Asian-American
> Poets*, edited by Joseph Bruchac.)

The annual American commemoration of Pearl Harbor offers as hateful a case history of racist miseducation according to the canon as any: Is there any other occasion on which the United States catapults into national acrobatics about having been caught off guard, caught by an enemy first strike?

If December 7, 1941, is "A Day of Infamy," what should we call August 6, 1945?

Why is the Japanese attack on Pearl Harbor so particularly galling and humiliating as to merit racist designation as a "Black Day" in American history?

Why do we remember Pearl Harbor and not V-J day? Why do we forget February 19, 1942, *that* Day of Infamy, when Franklin Roosevelt signed Executive Order 9066 whereby 100,000 innocent Japanese and Japanese-Americans were sentenced to American concentration camps? What is the difference between A Sneak Attack or A Terrorist Attack and, on the other hand, A Surprise Attack, A Brilliant Military Maneuver, A Pre-emptive Strike, or A Massive Allied Air Assault?

Is there a difference between the U.S. military base of Pearl Harbor and the Japanese civilian city of Hiroshima?

There is difference, and there is power. And who holds the power shall decide the meaning of difference.

Is there any difference between a wartime buddy of George Bush—a buddy flying a naval attack plane on a wartime mission against Japan—and 130,000 Japanese men, women, and children, civilians living in the civilian city of Hiroshima, where they were mass murdered, mass burned to death or deformed into a living death within five minutes of the United States' dropping the "Unthinkable Weapon," the atom bomb? Is there any difference?

What was the difference between official U.S. treatment accorded to German-Americans, Italian-Americans, and Japanese-Americans during World War II?

What's the difference between a German, an Italian, and somebody Japanese? Why were Germans and German-Americans and Italians and Italian-Americans *not* rounded up and sent to American concentration camps in World War II? Why were only those Japanese-Americans living on the West Coast sent to concentration camps?

Did you ever learn/did your teachers ever tell you that a higher percentage of Americans of Japanese ancestry ended up serving in the U.S. Army during World War II *than any other racial group*?

Did you know that until 1943 Federal law prohibited foreign-born Chinese from becoming American citizens?

Did you know that until 1952 Federal law prohibited foreign-born Japanese from becoming Americans?

Did you know that, having already segregated Chinese and Korean children, the San Francisco School Board in 1907 voted to segregate the total of the *100* Japanese children living there?

Is it possible that the Japanese government copped an attitude, at any point, toward the racist American policies and laws imposed upon Japanese people trying to live and work hard in the United States?

Question: Why am I always talking about racism, anyway?

Did you know that the Naturalization Act of 1790 decreed that only white people could become naturalized citizens of the United States?

Did you know that the Naturalization Act of 1790 fused all peoples of color into the damned and the despised and the legally unprotected American "underclass" now clamoring to overthrow The Canon that doesn't ever mention Hiroshima while it most certainly requires you to read Matthew Arnold, the Nineteenth Century poet, essayist, and arrogant jerk who pretty much invented White Poetry—or the notion of touchstones of Great Poetry—all of the touchstones being, as it happens, white male poets: Dante, Goethe, Pound, Eliot, Stevens, Heaney.

Because most well-educated Americans would have to answer, "I don't know" or "I didn't know" in response to that foregoing batch of test questions, a virulent Oreo phenomenon like Clarence Thomas becomes a probability rather than a shock.

And, on another level, Japan-bashing/Asian-bashing continues to flourish and intensify, even among other despised American groups who should know better.

How can anybody get past the ignorance that the American media and the academic canon guarantee?

It's not easy. A friend of mine, the preeminent scholar of Asian-American history, Ron Takaki, was told by Howard Goldberg of the *New York Times* that the *New York Times* was feeling "frankly over-Japanned." Moreover, Goldberg summarily dismissed Takaki as "dead wrong" because Takaki had dared to disagree with Goldberg about Pearl Harbor. Takaki had argued that there is both American and Japanese responsibility for that attack, and for the commencement of the Pacific war. Accordingly, Goldberg characterized Takaki's op-ed piece as "revisionist history" and, therefore, decided not to allow Takaki to appear on the *New York Times* op-ed page.

Education's overdue reform

It's not easy. But most Americans are not even distant relatives of the nice guys who run the country. And so there's not a lot of emotional blur to our perceptions. We've had to see them as clearly as the hunted need to watch the ones who hunt them down. Even without the overdue and radical reform of American education that sanity and democracy demand, some of us have learned more than we ever wanted to know about those nice guys.

Some of us sit in front of a young man, a member of the Creek nation, and we hear his voice break and we feel his hands trembling and we avoid staring at the tears that pour from his eyes as he tells us about the annihilation of his ancestors, about the bashing of babies' heads against trees, and about the alternate, nearly extinct worldview that his forefathers and foremothers embraced. Between convulsions of grief, he speaks about the loss of earlier, spirit relations between his hungering people and the foods of the Earth.

Some of us must devise and improvise a million and one ways to convince young African-American and Chicana women that white skin and yellow hair and blue eyes and thin thighs are not imperative attributes of beauty and loveliness.

Some of us must reassure a student born and raised in Hong Kong that we do not ask her to speak aloud in order to ridicule her "English" but in order to benefit from the wisdom of her intelligence.

Some of us search for avenues or for the invention of avenues for African-American boys to become men among men beyond and without surrendering to that racist offering of a kill-or-be-killed destiny.

And we move among the peoples of this nation on an eyeball basis. We do not deny the heterogeneity that surrounds our bodies and our minds. We do not suppress the variegated sounds of multiple languages spoken by so many truly different Americans all in one place, hoping for love.

I've been teaching a series of experimental poetry classes at the University of California-Berkeley. The enthusiastic, diverse, campus-wide student response led me to offer what I call Poetry for the People. Centered on student writings, this course publishes student poetry and presents these new poets in public readings of their work.

Traditional materials . . . have presented . . . every icon of knowledge required by "higher" education in the image of the powerful.

The ethnic, racial, intellectual, and sexual diversity of these students has forced me to attempt to devise a syllabus that is, for me, unprecedented, and even unwieldy, in its range. And for the first time I've had to ask for help from a diverse number of student teacher poets as well as other faculty, in order to handle the course materials responsibly.

The idea behind Poetry for the People is that every man or woman can be enabled to use language with the precision and the memorable impact that poetry requires. In this way, the writing and publishing and public presentation of poetry becomes a process of empowerment for students as well as a catalyst for coalition politics of a practical and spontaneous nature.

Student readings have been attended by standing-room-only crowds, without exception. Required books for the course include Native American, Chicana/Chicano, white poetry, African-American poetry, women's poetry, Asian-American poetry.

And so I am trying to become Politically Correct. I am just one among an expanding hard-core number of American educators who believe that an American culture requirement, for instance, is not a laughable or subversive or anti-intellectual proposal: On the contrary! We are teachers running as fast as we can to catch up with the new Americans we are paid to educate.

In 1987, the Hudson Institute released a report entitled "Workforce 2000." According to the *San Francisco Chronicle* "the report stunned American business leaders with its projection that in the remaining years of this century, *only 15 per cent of the entrants into the workforce would be white males.*" (My italics.)

That's nationwide.

By the year 2010, California's population will nearly double, and this will be the racial breakdown: overall, 61 per cent people of color; 39 per cent non-Hispanic white; 38 per cent Hispanic; 16 per cent Asian; 7 per cent black.

From that total population, we will have to publicly educate nearly twice as many students as the total number in 1991. What will we teach these new Americans? How will we seek to justify every lecture, every homework assignment?

In 1992 this was the composition of the freshman class at UC-Berkeley, reputedly the best public university in the United States: 30 per cent white; 31.5 per cent Asian; 20.5 per cent Hispanic; 7.5 per cent black; i.e.. 59.5 per cent people of color.

And so, walking across this American campus, you will see, as I have seen, on an eyeball basis, that this America of ours is changing faster than fast—although the faculty at Berkeley remains 89 per cent white, which represents only a 2 per cent decrease of white faculty members during the last ten years.

The current distribution and identity of power will have to change, as well, or we will have to laugh the word *democracy* out of our consciousness forever.

And that is the political crisis that each of us personifies, one way or the other:

Since the demographics of our nation state do not even forecast English as the usual first language of most of our future children, what is the meaning of "English Only" legislation, for example, in the state of California?

What does that reveal besides the politics of culture?

And who shall decide what these many peoples of America shall know or not know?

And what does that question underscore besides the political nature of knowledge?

And what shall be the international identity and what shall be the national identity of these United States when a white majority no longer exists inside our boundaries even as a white majority has never existed beyond these blood-and-gore-begotten boundaries of our nation state?

I do not agree that I am a statistical component of some alarming controversy. The indisputable value of each and every one of our lives is not debatable, is not politically correct or incorrect.

The annual American commemoration of Pearl Harbor offers as hateful a case history of racist miseducation according to the canon as any.

In this crisis of American power, in this conflict between power and human life, *there can be no canon, there can be no single text for the education of our multicultural, multilingual, multiracial population!*

Some thirty years ago, in his "Letter to My Nephew," James Baldwin wrote the following:

"Know whence you came. If you know whence you came, there is really no limit to where you can go. The details and symbols of our life have been deliberately constructed to make you believe what white people say about you. Please try to remember that what they believe, as well as what they do and cause you to endure, does not testify to your inferiority but to their inferiority and fear."

And, in that same letter, he wrote: "If the word *integration* means anything, this is what it means: That we, with love, shall force our brothers to see themselves as they are, to cease fleeing from reality and begin to change it."

And so I propose that we undertake to make of the teachings of public education in America a politically correct, a verifiably sane basis for our multicultural, multiracial, and two-gendered lives on this infinitely multifaceted, multilingual planet. I propose that we undertake this awesome work with imperturbable pride and, yes, fanatical zeal.

It seems to me that this moment of ours is just an obvious, excellent moment to declare for Americans, and for ourselves, a Manifest New Destiny: a destiny that will extricate all of us from the sickness of egomania and ignorance, a destiny that will cherish and delight in the differences among us, a destiny that will depend upon empowerment of the many and merciful protection of the young and the weak, a destiny that will carry us beyond an eyeball basis of knowledge into an educated, collective vision of a really democratic, a really humane, a really really good time together.

7

Resisting a Multicultural Curriculum

Rush H. Limbaugh III

Rush H. Limbaugh III is a popular conservative commentator and the author of The Way Things Ought to Be, *which appeared on the* New York Times *best-sellers list for more than a year, and* See, I Told You So, *which had the largest first printing (two million copies) in history. Limbaugh hosts nationally syndicated radio and television shows, each with an audience of approximately twenty million.*

What is being taught in schools as multiculturalism is worse than historical revisionism and more than a distortion of facts. It is the elimination of facts that document Western civilization's achievements. If ethnic subcultures have genuine vitality, they will be instilled in children by families, churches, and communities, and will not need to be taught in schools. For true integration to occur, Americans must celebrate their common culture and work toward blending into a harmonious society. Stressing multiculturalism will promote separatism and heighten ethnic tensions. The bonds of national cohesion are fragile enough as it is. Public education should strengthen, not weaken, these bonds.

A few years ago, radical students at Stanford University protested against a required course in the great texts of Western civilization. They organized a march, led by the Reverend Jesse Jackson, with a chant, "Hey, hey, ho, ho, Western culture's gotta go." And Stanford capitulated and abolished the Western civilization requirement. It was replaced with watered-down courses in which books were supposed to be examined from the perspective of "race, class, and gender," and readings from St. Augustine and John Locke were interspersed with such works as the autobiography of Guatemalan Marxist guerrilla fighter Rigoberta Menchu and a documentary on Navajo Indians entitled "Our Cosmos, Our Sheep, Our Bodies, Ourselves."

Multiculturalism is billed as a way to make Americans more sensitive to the diverse cultural backgrounds of people in this country. It's time we blew the whistle on that. What is being taught under the guise of multiculturalism is worse than historical revisionism; it's more than a distortion of facts; it's an elimination of facts. In some schools, kids are being taught that the ideas of the Constitution were really borrowed from the Iroquois Indians, and that Africans discovered America by crossing the Atlantic on rafts hundreds of years before Columbus and made all sorts of other scientific discoveries and inventions that were later stolen from them. They are told that the ancient Greeks and Romans stole all of their ideas from the Egyptians and that the Egyptians were black Africans.

In fact, most historians and anthropologists will tell you that while there was a lot of cultural exchange in the ancient world and the Greeks and Romans absorbed some of the Egyptian ideas, it was only one of many influences. And the ancient Egyptians were dark-skinned but not black, even though many scholars have been so intimidated that they will only say this off the record. My purpose here is not to be critical of Africans or African culture, but simply to point out that not one syllable of any of our founding documents can be traced to the roots of tribal Africa—and that neither I nor anyone else is going to improve racial relations by pretending otherwise.

American culture

There is a fallacious premise out there that black kids have low self-esteem because they don't have any roots. They don't have anything to relate to in their past except slavery and degradation, and to elevate their self-esteem we must teach them about the great cultures of their ancestors. I think the multiculturalists are perpetrating a tremendous and harmful fraud when they take young black kids in public schools and teach them things that are irrelevant or even counterproductive to their future as Americans. They teach that street slang is just as good as grammatical English, that whites are cold and logical but blacks are warm and intuitive, and that Africans have a different approach to numbers that doesn't emphasize precision. Well, if you want to get a job with IBM you've got to have the skills that will help you get that job. And that involves a lot of things. Not just the skills, such as logical thinking and mathematics, but language, appearance, showing up on time. And if the kids have been taught that learning these things means compromising themselves and conforming to white values, how on earth can they be expected to succeed? If you want to prosper in America, if you want access to opportunity in America, you must be able to assimilate: to become part of the American culture. Just as in any other country of the world—if an American moved there, he would have to adapt to its culture if he wanted to succeed. The so-called minorities in this country are not being done any favors when the multiculturalist crowd forces their attitudinal segregation from mainstream society. The politics of cultural pride are actually the politics of alienation, in a different uniform.

Americans have always seemed to pride themselves in describing theirs as a melting-pot culture, where everyone is welcome and all will be treated equally. There is no question that this country has severe blemishes in its past (slavery) with respect to equality of treatment and access to opportunity. But the way for us to overcome that, in my opinion, is to strive toward racial color-blindness, rather than to encourage members of different cultures, especially their youth during their formative years, to dwell on their native cultures. I believe I have a consistent position here because I certainly do not advocate the schools' focusing on a historical review of my ancestry either. For America to truly arrive as an integrated society, we have to begin behaving as though we are all Americans; that we have a culture ourselves, and that all of the various cultures that compose our great nation should work toward blending into a harmonious society. It can be argued that such a position is easy for a white man in this country. To that I can only respond that I admit that racism continues to exist in every imaginable direction among all races. But we are certainly more likely to make inroads against those attitudes and make progress toward actual equality if we learn to view one another as human beings; not as blacks, African-Americans, WASPS, Jews, Native Americans, Asians, or Latinos.

What is this American culture toward which we should all aspire? American culture is defined primarily by the idea of self-reliance. That's how this country was built: people of every background fending for themselves and for their families. And it's something we are losing. If you tell someone to get a job, you are using dirty words now; you are being insensitive. Now you are told to define yourself by your place within a tribe or a group. People have accused me of racism or insensitivity when I challenge the multiculturalist view on history and education. But far from being a racist, far from being a bigot, I have a great deal of compassion and love for people of all backgrounds, and I also love my country. I want this to be a great country, and a great country needs as many great individuals as there can be. These young black kids in public schools in America are Americans. Not Africans, not Jamaicans, but Americans. And we have to treat them as such. It is in our nation's best interest, and in their best interest too, for them to grow up as good Americans, to know American culture, to learn to prosper in America. And I have that hope. I want everyone to be taught the things that are necessary for them to prosper as Americans, not black something or brown something or red something, but as Americans.

The multiculturalist movement

Of course there are people in the multiculturalist movement who have the best of intentions, who think the movement is dedicated to helping members of minority cultures become more well rounded. And I don't want to castigate all advocates of multiculturalism. In fact, if people want to teach ancient African history, or Third World cultures, or women's studies, that's fine—as long as it doesn't become the primary perspective and doesn't supplant the things that all American kids need to know— and as long as it is not coupled with the fraudulent message that the minorities' best opportunity of succeeding in this society is to jealously cling to their past.

The historian Arthur Schlesinger, whose book *The Disuniting of America* was published [in 1991], writes that if ethnic subcultures have genuine vitality, they will be instilled in children by families, churches, and communities. The children will not need encouragement from the schools to learn about their ethnicity and their heritage, to learn their language, and so forth. If the communities do not instill these things in their children, then it's obviously not a very important part of their lives to begin with. So, there must be some other motives behind the drive for multiculturalism than making children aware of their heritage.

Multiculturalism is primarily—though not exclusively—a tool of black educators and of those sympathetic to the injustices blacks have suffered and continue to suffer in America. There is a feeling that blacks will never be able to make it if they have to play by the same rules, because America is so flawed and American culture is so racist and prejudiced. But there's something I'd like to know. How is it that boatloads of Vietnamese people, without any prior exposure to American culture or any knowledge of the English language, can arrive on the West Coast and, seven years later or less, speak the language fluently, run prosperous businesses, and have their kids scoring near the top in our schools? In California, the Asians are outperforming everyone else on college entrance exams—so much so that the University of California actually has instituted quotas on admissions of Asian-Americans, because otherwise many whites and blacks wouldn't get in. I'm sure many blacks and whites are embarrassed by this. And the fact is that I don't see these Asian-Americans getting any special Asian-studies courses in high school or grade school to boost their self-esteem. No one is setting up Vietnamese-history courses for these kids—and they seem to be doing just fine anyway.

Why is that? In my opinion, it is primarily because their families came here, intact, to escape oppression in their own countries and to take advantage of the opportunities that America offers. They are not told that they should be bitter about America and that they should dwell on the study of their own cultures. They come here to join in the culture and to succeed within the rules, not to change the rules. And it's not just the Vietnamese but people from other Asian countries and blacks from the West Indies and from Africa who are seeking to come here. On the other hand, many people who were born here have the attitude that they shouldn't be required to make an effort to educate themselves and get themselves out of poverty—society owes it to them, as compensation for the injustices perpetrated against their grandparents. For the black leadership to continue to encourage their people to absorb themselves in the past, instead of helping them get beyond the bitterness, is doing them a great disservice.

Of course, the argument is that black Americans are different from all other groups. They didn't choose to come here; their ancestors were brought here in slave ships. I won't deny that, nor will I defend this country's original sin. But there's nothing we can do about it now. It may not be fair, but we can't change the past. Black Americans are here. The only solution, as I said, is for blacks to be treated as Americans, to be taught the things they need to know as Americans, and to be held to the same standards as other Americans. I realize that my suggestion that we encourage assimilation rather than alienation is easier said than done. But an overhauling of our attitudes toward one another, so as to de-emphasize rather than to emphasize our cultural differences, will do far more in the long run to advance the plight of minorities, than will the artificial remedy of reverse discrimination.

On fairness

Now let's talk about fairness for a moment. I get frustrated listening to all this talk about fairness. And it's not restricted to multiculturalism. We demand a fair and level playing field in foreign trade, for example. But are we going to get it just because we demand it? You have to deal with things as they are; that's one of the earliest lessons kids need to be taught.

Things in life are not always going to be fair. Even John Kennedy said life isn't fair. Yes, the Japanese won't import our products, but that has nothing to do with why Americans don't buy American-made goods. The Japanese aren't playing fair but that's not why some of our products are inferior. There is no causal relationship there. So in formulating our solutions to this problem we shouldn't allow our emotions to interfere with our good judgment.

Here's another example: After I was on *The Phil Donahue Show*, my rabid fans, God love them all, started calling and saying, "Rush, you were great but gee, we felt sorry for you. He wasn't fair to you. He didn't let you finish your sentences, he tried to misrepresent what you said, he took you out of context. He was so mean." And I said, "What did you expect? It's Phil Donahue. He's a liberal, I'm a conservative. Were you surprised by anything he did? Well, neither was I." When they invited me to be on, do you think I said, "All right, but only if he's nice, only if he's fair?" No, I went into the arena knowing the ground rules and fully anticipating the treatment I was to receive. I had seen *The Phil Donahue Show*, I knew what it was like. If I had had an affair with my wife's mother and sister, or if I were castrated and still afraid of the bicycle bar, I would have been occupying the moral high ground on Donahue's turf. But I went in there as a conservative, and I knew I would be persona non grata; I knew it was going to be rough. And I think I handled it superbly. I didn't let Donahue get away with distorting my views, although he did a masterful job trying. The point I am trying to make is that if you insist on fairness before you do anything, you're never going to get anything done.

I want everyone to be taught the things that are necessary for them to prosper as Americans, not black something or brown something or red something.

Multiculturalism is based upon the premise that there is such terrible unfairness out there that minority cultures can't triumph over it. All of us are constantly exposed to a barrage of negative news. We are told that misery has finally taken over in America, that the American dream is dead. And what I find especially appalling is that so many people seem to be happy that misery persists, because it enables them to say, "I told you so." If you agree that misery is everywhere and you wallow in it, then you are caring and compassionate. If you encourage people to extricate themselves from it, you are told that you are uncaring. If a minority member succeeds in bettering himself, he is resented by those who haven't. Clarence Thomas and Michael Jordan are among those who are sometimes accused of abandoning their roots to succeed in the white man's world. Because Clarence Thomas worked hard and was able to rise from an impoverished background, to play by the rules of American society and succeed, he was accused of being uncaring and insensitive toward his fellow blacks who had not escaped poverty. Success means an automatic inability to relate. How ironic it is that the black leadership purports to stand for the betterment of its people, but when its people do succeed they are immediately outcast. Here, try this: Soon after the final episode of *The Cosby Show*, a group of black sociologists released the results of a "study" they had conducted of the show. Their conclusion: *The Cosby*

Show, by portraying blacks as successful, upwardly mobile residents of the middle class, sent the wrong message to both blacks and whites. What message? Why, the nonsense that blacks can make it in America if only they try. So there you have it—again. Black success is to be denied, is not even to be portrayed, because it does not happen. Well, it does happen, and often. The largest percentage of the 29 million black people in America—67 percent—are middle and upper-middle class.

Propagandists of multiculturalism

It is my conviction that the people who concocted multiculturalism and are now trying to institute a multicultural curriculum in New York are basically miserable. And rather than look at their own responsibility in this, or try to find solutions that involve a change in attitudes, they simply blame institutions. They blame America. So multiculturalism, which portrays American history and even all of Western civilization as nothing but misery and racist, sexist, capitalist oppression, is the tool of revenge of many who have failed to assimilate and fit into mainstream American life. And the primary targets of their revenge are our children. They are taking it out on our kids by filling their minds with mush and teaching them how horrible America is.

Look at all the attacks on Christopher Columbus in [the] quincentennial year of 1992. There's no question that Christopher Columbus was a major historical figure. You can say what you want about some of the things he did, but he certainly changed the course of history. The tribes that populated America when he arrived did not change the course of history. The Vikings who sailed to America did not change the course of history. Columbus did.

Now, five hundred years later, in history classes where multiculturalism has reared its ugly head, and also in books, in the media, and let's not forget Hollywood, Christopher Columbus is being portrayed as a mean, vicious, cruel monster. He was probably a racist, a sexist, a homophobe, and a bigot.

He chopped off the hands of natives in the West Indies and in the Caribbean, he took slaves, he originated the plundering of the environment—he did all kinds of horrible, evil things. People are saying, "Columbus! White male Europeans, they're the cause of the problems we're having today."

What I really love to see is the propagandists of multiculturalism getting caught in their own trap. Recently, some historians were speculating that Columbus might not deserve credit for discovering the New World after all, because it may have been Columbus's wife who told him which course to take. The new theory was that he was going to sail in the other direction, but his wife (her name was probably Hillary) said, "No, go that way." So, you see, it was his wife, obviously one of the pioneering feminists in America, telling her husband what to do and which way to go, who is responsible for America's discovery by the Europeans. This is bizarre. Feminists are in league with multiculturalists, saying that white European males are the problem, and now we learn that perhaps the first feminist in the world sent Columbus here! So the feminists are responsible for the advent of Western civilization in this land, and all its attendant evils. Now, that's justice.

But let's get back to Columbus. All right, just for the sake of argument, let's say that the Columbus-bashers are right. Let's say he was as evil as they make him out to be and that he committed all those horrible things of which they accuse him, and more. Let's even stipulate that he is related to [former Los Angeles police chief] Daryl Gates. Would somebody please tell me where, in the founding documents of the United States of America, there is anything based on Christopher Columbus's beliefs, or his actions, or his philosophy? It just isn't there. The American system of government did not come from Columbus.

Multiculturalism . . . is the tool of revenge of many who have failed to assimilate and fit into mainstream American life.

But that's not the way the multiculturalists see it. To them, it's the single best way to get at easily influenced young minds and tear the country down. If the man who discovered America is flawed, if he's a bad guy, then everything that followed from that discovery has to be immoral—the fruit of the poisonous tree. In the same way, we are told that because George Washington and Thomas Jefferson held slaves, and because Jefferson supposedly had a sexual relationship with one of his female slaves—which is a lie to begin with—the constitutional system of government that they created is tainted. But it's not just the kids who are being spoon-fed these lies. So are we adults. And we're not challenging it. What happened to our backbone?

No one can convince me that the point of all this is not to discredit all that America stands for—and the ultimate goal, I firmly believe, is the destruction of the capitalist way of life, the destruction of free enterprise, and the establishment of socialism, because socialism to these people equals fairness. De Tocqueville observed, "Democracy and socialism have nothing in common but one word: equality. But notice the difference: while democracy seeks equality in liberty, socialism seeks equality in restraint and servitude."

When you look at what's being taught in the schools today, as Dr. Schlesinger has shown, the primary culture of America is being ripped apart, criticized, denigrated, and people are being told to look to their ancient ethnic roots for salvation and goodness.

If you think about it, multiculturalism flies in the face of what this country is all about. This country was built by people who were fleeing the oppression of the societies in which they were born. You know, there is something to those old cliches about America being a beacon of hope and prosperity. These may be cliches but they really are true. When there's a food shortage anywhere in the world, where do those suffering go for help? The United States. When somebody needs technology, where do they go? The United States. When somebody needs a donation, a handout, a loan, they come to the United States. And when somebody wants to escape oppression, where do they go? The United States. The people fleeing Haiti did not go to St. Thomas or to Cuba. They tried to come to the United States.

The reason all those people from different countries have been coming to America is that America is different from the countries they left. America offers individual freedom and the opportunity to make something of yourself. But multiculturalism is the exact opposite of that. We are now supposed to teach these people the values and the alleged virtues of the oppressive societies which they fled, rather than the values and virtues of the free society they sought. Please cogitate on that for a moment. We're even trying to teach it to the kids who never lived in those oppressive societies—we're supposed to teach them to champion the very things their parents escaped, many of them risking their lives in the process.

Let me say it again: Ethnic communities that are committed to preserving some of their cultural values and their heritage should be free to instill these values in their children—at home, at church, in the neighborhood. Surely it is not the office of public schools to promote separatism and heighten ethnic tensions. The bonds of national cohesion in the republic are fragile enough as it is. Public education's aim should be to strengthen, not weaken, them.

8
America Should Strengthen Its European Cultural Roots

Russell Kirk

Russell Kirk (1918-1994), author of The American Cause *and* The Roots of American Order, *was one of America's most preeminent conservative thinkers and writers. He was a distinguished scholar at the Heritage Foundation, a Washington, D.C., conservative think tank.*

America's common culture is derived from European—especially British—institutions and concepts, and is the ideal culture for all Americans to emulate. But this inherited order is threatened by decay and multiculturalism. Long before the ideology of multiculturalism, American schools taught much about the diversity of international cultures. But American schooling deteriorated over time; children grew up unicultural and ignorant of other countries and societies. Multiculturalism today, however, offers no solutions. It is anti-cultural, animated by envy and hatred, and does nothing more than gratify ethnic vanities. Multiculturalists threaten to destroy the nation's elaborate existing culture. The guardians of Anglo-American culture must resist this threat and reinvigorate America's higher culture.

What is called *order*, a word signifying harmonious arrangement, has two aspects when we discuss the diverse cultures of humankind. The first of these is order in the soul: what is called moral order. The second of these is order in the commonwealth: what is called constitutional order. In both its aspects, order stands endangered today, requiring vigorous defense.

Six decades ago in *The Revolt of the Masses*, José Ortega y Gasset wrote that American civilization could not long survive any catastrophe to European society. This remains true, and particularly true with respect to Britain. America's higher culture, and the American civil social order, are derived from institutions and concepts that arose to the east of the Atlantic Ocean. Americans are part of a great continuity and essence.

America and Britain and their cultural dependencies share a common religious heritage, a common history in large part, a common pattern of law and politics, and a common body of great literature. Yet American cit-

Russell Kirk, "The Fraud of Multiculturalism," *The Heritage Lecture Series*, no. 396, May 29, 1992. Copyrighted by and reprinted by permission of The Heritage Foundation, Washington, D.C.

izens and British subjects cannot be wholly confident that their order will endure forever. It is possible to exhaust moral and social capital; a society relying altogether upon its patrimony soon may find itself bankrupt. With civilization, as with the human body, conservation and renewal are possible only if healthful change and reinvigoration occur from age to age. It is by no means certain that our present moral and constitutional order is providing sufficiently for its own future. Modern men pay a great deal of attention to material and technological means, but little attention to the instruments by which any generation must fulfill its part in the contract of eternal society.

Grim symptoms

Twentieth century mankind, in Britain and in America, have tended to be contemptuous of the past; yet they contribute little enough of their own, except in technology and applied sciences, toward the preservation of a tolerable order, let alone its improvement. The facile optimism of the nineteenth and early twentieth centuries is much diminished nowadays, but this does not signify that naive notions of inevitable Progress have been supplanted by serious reflection on the problem of how to conserve and to renew our cultural patrimony. The present threat to the inner order and the outer order comes as much from indifference, empathy, and selfishness as it comes from totalist political powers. Pessimism for pessimism's sake is as fatuous as is optimism for optimism's sake. Grim symptoms may be discerned of an absolute decline of the higher culture in both America and Britain, and also symptoms of a decline of the ties that have joined the English-speaking cultures on either side of the Atlantic. How may decay be arrested?

In any age, some people revolt against their own inheritance of order—and soon find themselves plunged into what Edmund Burke called "the antagonist world of madness, discord, vice, confusion, and unavailing sorrow." Near the end of the twentieth century, the number of such enemies to order has become alarming. A spirit of defiance or biting criticism that may be healthful, when confined to a creative minority, can become perilous if it is taken up unimaginatively by a popular majority. To the folk who rebel against their patrimony of moral and constitutional order, that legacy seems a burden—when in truth it is a footing. Cultural restoration, like charity, begins at home; and so I touch here upon symptoms of neglect of the common inheritance of America.

Religious faith, whether Catholic, Protestant, or Judaic, seems enfeebled in the United States. Many of the clergy tend markedly toward a sentimental and humanitarian application of religious teachings; they incline toward the radical alteration of society at the expense of the transcendent ends of religion and of any personal obedience to moral teachings.

As for the legacy of ordered liberty, there, too, one finds cause for misgiving. Even among judges and lawyers, one encounters a growing disregard of the old principles of justice and jurisprudence; and one encounters, too, an overwhelming tendency toward concentration of power in centralized governments.

The causes of such drifts may be found, in part, in the gradual substitution of "pragmatic" standards for old principles of jurisprudence and inherited political institutions. With few exceptions, schools of law have encouraged this progress. There may come to pass the triumph of what Eric

Voegelin called "theoretical illiteracy" in law and politics. A university student of considerable native intelligence inquires of me why checks and balances are at all desirable in politics. Why should we not simply train up an elite of governmental administrators, he inquires, trust to their good will and abilities, and let them manage the concerns of the nation?

This growing naïveté, born of an ignorance of the political and legal institutions of the British-American culture, too often passes unchallenged by disciples of the pragmatic and technical methodologies dominant in schools of public administration and in governmental research. This simplicity also reflects a wondrous unawareness of human nature and of statecraft. It is the attitude that Lord Percy of Newcastle denominated "totalist democracy"—a trust in an abstraction called The People, combined with an unquestioning faith in The Expert.

Grim symptoms may be discerned of an absolute decline of the higher culture in both America and Britain.

Theoretical illiteracy in politics and jurisprudence is paralleled by a decline of true apprehension of humane letters. In the Anglo-American culture, the study of great literature has pursued an ethical end through an intellectual means. The improvement of reason and conscience for the person's own sake, and the incidental improvement of society thereby, was the object of the traditional literary disciplines. The present generation of schoolchildren is expected, instead, to "learn to live with all the world, in one global village"—a consummation to be achieved, perhaps, by scissors-and-paste projects.

When poetry is replaced by "communication skills" and narrative history by vague sociological generalizations, the intricate patrimony of general culture is threatened. There exist professors of education who argue that no young person ought to read any book more than half a century old. The imaginative and rational disciplines, so painfully cultivated over centuries, can be permanently injured by a generation or two of neglect and contempt.

Modern men and women live in an age in which the expectation of change often seems greater than the expectation of continuity. In any order worthy of the name, men and women must be something better than the flies of a summer, generation must link with generation. Some people, in this closing decade of the twentieth century, are doing what is in their power to preserve a common heritage. This is not a work that can be accomplished through fresh positive laws or through the creation of new international commissions. Yet if a people forget the ashes of their fathers and the temples of their gods, the consequences soon will be felt in the laws and in international affairs. Cultural continuity lacking, there remains small point in political tinkering with a body social that has become exhausted spiritually and intellectually.

A French aphorism instructs us that the more things change, the more they are the same. We fight over again, generation after generation, the battle to maintain the inner order and the outer. As T. S. Eliot wrote, there are no lost causes because there are no gained causes. Say not the struggle naught availeth. In defense of the order into which we have been born, one may reaffirm the counsel of Edgar, in *King Lear:*

> Take heed o' th' foul fiend; obey thy parents; keep thy word justly;
> swear not; commit not with man's sworn spouse; set not thy sweet
> heart on proud array. . . . Keep thy foot out of brothel, thy hand
> out of placket, thy pen from lender's book, and defy the foul fiend.

From Shakespeare, as from other most memorable dead, comes the
energy that sustains people in a time of tribulation. The order, inner and
outer, of our common culture is defended not by the living merely, but
by the valiant dead as well.

Challenge and response

From time to time, during this twentieth century, some American voices
have been raised in dispraise of America's inheritance of British culture.
One such assault occurred about the middle forties; it was renewed a
decade later. Even some American scholars of good repute suggest that it
would be well to drop from formal instruction most of our baggage of
British literature, and to concentrate instead upon native American verse
and prose; certain language associations embrace this line; buy the home-
grown product! In effect these literary nationalists advocate a cultural
Tariff of Abominations.

Dr. Louis B. Wright, then director of the Folger Shakespeare Library
in Washington, took up his cudgel about 1952 in defense of a civilized
heritage, against academic allies of barbarism. In his lively book *Culture
on the Moving Frontier*, Dr. Wright repeatedly and persuasively digressed
from his narrative to point out the essentially British character of American institutions and the American realm of reason and of art. He wrote in
his first chapter:

> Modern America is so polyglot, and social historians have devoted
> so much attention in recent years to analyzing and describing the
> multifarious European, Asiatic, and African influences in the de-
> velopment of American life that we are now in danger of underes-
> timating and even forgetting the oldest, the most persistent, and
> the most vigorous strain in our cultural inheritance. Great Britain's
> influence is still so strong that it subtly determines qualities of
> mind and character in Americans who cannot claim a drop of
> Anglo-Saxon blood. . . . If there were no other legacy from the past
> except the English language and its literature, that alone would be
> sufficient to explain the durability and strength of the tradition.

Four decades after Professor Wright reproved thus the Goths and
Vandals within the Ivory Tower, a new horde of adversaries is bent upon
deconstructing the edifice of Anglo-American culture. The principal ac-
crediting associations of the United States, indeed, have menaced colleges
and universities with disaccreditation unless they promptly proceed to
enter upon programs of multiculturalism, permeating the whole curriculum. And various academic presidents and deans have supinely submit-
ted to this intellectual bullying; but the federal Secretary of Education has
rebuffed these barbarous educationists somewhat, threatening *them* in
turn with governmental disaccreditation of unjust accreditors.

One encounters in today's American education, truly, a great deal of
dullness, at every level; and much intellectual provinciality, too. Ever since
the Second World War, indeed, oddly enough, American schooling, from
kindergarten through graduate school, has sunk farther and farther into

the provinciality of place and time, so that the rising generation grows up unicultural, notably ignorant of other countries and other cultures, despite the tremendous ascendancy of the United States in world affairs.

A multicultural curriculum

Six decades ago, when I was enrolled in a public grade school not far from great railway yards outside Detroit, nobody thought of demanding multiculturalism: we already possessed that in our school. In geography class, we learned a great deal about the cultures of five continents; we were very interested. Many of us, a few years later, enrolled (during high school) in three years of history: ancient, modern, and American. At least half of us took two years of language, either Latin or French, with corresponding instruction about Roman civilization or French culture; some pupils finished four years of foreign language. Our intelligent courses in English and American literature helped to redeem us from what T. S. Eliot called "the provincialism of time." We were much aware of diversity in the world and in our own country.

Today the radical multiculturalists complain, or rather shout, that African, Asian, and Latin American cultures have been shamefully neglected in North America's schools. In that they are correct enough. In many primary, intermediate, and high schools nowadays—aye, in colleges, too—the offering in the discipline of history amounts only to a whirlwind "Survey of World History" (with Good Guys and Bad Guys occasionally pointed out by the teacher, amidst the violent dust storm), and perhaps a year of American history, often ideologically distorted. As for geography, that virtually has gone by the board; at least one famous state university, a few years ago, swept away altogether its department of geography. Even at boarding schools of good repute and high fees, the teaching of humane letters is very nearly confined to reading and discussing some recent ephemeral novels.

What the curious sect of multiculturalists prescribe, in Britain as in America, is poison.

Sixty years ago, most school pupils were taught a good deal about the people and the past of Bolivia, Morocco, China, India, Egypt, Guatemala, and other lands. They even learnt about Eskimo and Aleut cultures. Nowadays pupils are instructed in the disciplines of sexology, driver education, sex education, and the sterile abstractions of Social Studies. Formerly all pupils studied for several years the principal British and American poets, essayists, and novelists and dramatists—this with the purpose of developing their moral imagination. Nowadays they are assigned the prose of "relevance" and "current awareness" at most schools. Indeed a great deal of alleged "education," either side of the Ocean Sea, requires medication or surgery.

But what the curious sect of multiculturalists prescribe, in Britain as in America, is poison. There is reason to suspect that such multiculturalists as Leonard Jeffries, a black radical professor at the City College of New York, hope to bring down the whole edifice of pedagogy—so as to hold among the ruins perpetual "rap sessions" about indignities once suffered by blacks.[1]

Yet suppose that the multiculturalists were sincere in their professions of desire to redress the balance by reducing emphases upon Eurocentric and British culture, and introducing new programs to describe other cultures that have affected the United States—why, how might the thing be accomplished? The number of hours in an academic day is limited. How would a multicultural curriculum deal with the worthy contributions of Armenians, Syrians, Lebanese, Iraqi Chaldeans, Russians, Ukrainians, Poles, Serbs, Maltese, Croats, Puerto Ricans, Czechs, Chinese, Vietnamese, Mexicans, Hungarians, and a score of other "minorities" that inhabit the city of Detroit, say? Early in 1991, the Detroit School Board instructed publishers of textbooks that the Board would give short shrift to any school manuals that did not fully emphasize the contributions of Afro-Americans to American culture. Are textbooks for instruction, or are they to become merely devices for "increasing the self-esteem" of ethnic groups?

Whims of minorities

Even before multiculturalism was taken seriously by anybody, it was sufficiently difficult to publish a textbook that objectively dealt with its subject. A decade ago, I was editing a series of social science manuals. In a history textbook, it had been found prudent to insert a chapter on the Mongols—giving those devastators equal space and classroom time with Hellenes and Romans. In that chapter appeared the phrase "the charge of the barbarian horsemen." Our textbooks were printed and distributed by a commercial textbook publisher, acting for our council. A woman editor of that firm instructed me, "There may have been women among them. Change your phrase to 'the charge of the barbarian horsepersons.'" I replied to her that in historical fact, the ferocious cavalry of Genghis Khan included no females; and that I knew of no American woman who would be gratified by being labelled a "barbarian horseperson." Such are the difficulties that arise when objective scholarship is subject to the whims of all "minorities"—and, moreover, those "minorities" are engaged in endless warfare, one against another.

It is well to learn much about distant cultures. When a sophomore in college, this writer spent a whole year reading rare works about travels in Africa, borrowed from the shelves of the Library of the State of Michigan—considerably to the neglect of the conventional disciplines for which he was being graded at his college. But to neglect or to repudiate the central and pervasive British culture in America would be to let the whole academic and social enterprise fall apart, "The center cannot hold; mere anarchy is loosed upon the world. . . . "

To deny "minorities" the benefits of America's established culture would work their ruin.

May the Anglo-American culture, so battered by the pace of change during the twentieth century, so damaged by ideological assaults these past several decades, be restored to health? (It is one culture, really, that complex of literature and law and government and mores which still makes civilization possible in both the United States and Britain. Of the three major poets in the English language during the twentieth century— T. S. Eliot, Robert Frost, William Butler Yeats—two were American born, a fact suggesting that British and American cultures have coalesced.) No culture endures forever: Of those that have vanished, some have fallen to alien conquerors, as did Roman Britain; but most have expired in consequence of internal decay. When the cult failed, the culture presently crumbled to powder. Will the American culture and the British expire jointly "not with a bang, but a whimper"? One thinks of the Chorus in Sir Osbert Sitwell' s long poem "Demos the Emperor":

> We are the modern masters of the world,
> The arbiters, the heirs
> Of Egypt, Greece and Italy
> (We have no time for art
> But we know what we like!)
> We are the fulfillment of Man' s Promise
> The Cup-tie Final and the paper cap;
> We are the Soul of the Cash Register,
> The Secret of the Hire-Purchase System,
> The Vacuum, and the Vacuum-Cleaner.[2]

As I once remarked to President Richard Nixon, great cultures commonly pass through alternating periods of decay and renewal, flickering out finally after many centuries. Byzantine civilization is our clearest instance of this process. The culture from which Anglo-American culture developed extends back more than three thousand years, to Moses and Aaron. Cultures cannot be deliberately created; they arise, rather, from the theophanic events that bring cults into existence. It remains conceivable, nevertheless, that cultures may be *reinvigorated*.

Watering the roots

If America's British culture is to be reinvigorated, its roots must be watered. The twentieth century guardians of that culture must reject such silliness as the multiculturalist ideology, which does nothing more than gratify little ethnic vanities. Those guardians—who are the whole class of tolerably educated Americans—must resist those ideologues of multiculturalism who would pull down the whole elaborate existing culture of this country in order to make everybody culturally equal—that is equal in ignorance. On this point, Louis B. Wright deserves to be quoted a final time:

> For better or for worse, we have inherited the fundamental quali-ties in our culture from the British. For that reason we need to take a long perspective of our history, a perspective which views Amer-ica from at least the period of the first Tudor monarchs and lets us see the gradual development of our common civilization, its trans-mission across the Atlantic, and its expansion and modification as it was adapted to conditions in the Western Hemisphere. We should not overlook other influences which have affected Ameri-can life, influences from France, Holland, Spain, Germany, Scandi-navia, and the rest of Europe, and also influences from Asia and Africa. But we must always remember that such was the vigor of British culture that it assimilated all others. That is not to say that we have been transmogrified into Englishmen, or that we are even Anglophile in sentiment. But we cannot escape an inheritance which has given us some of our sturdiest and most lasting qualities.

Arnold Toynbee instructs us that cultures develop, and civilizations arise, by the process of challenge and response. Some threat to a culture's survival may occur; if that culture vigorously surmounts that challenge, the culture will grow in strength. But if the challenge is so formidable as to damage or distort the culture—why, the threatened culture becomes stunted and possibly succumbs altogether.

The ideology called multiculturalism might benefit American society, after all—in the sense that it is a challenge (if a foolish challenge) to the friends of America's inherited culture. If the response to the multiculturalist threat is healthy, it should rouse again among Americans an apprehension of the high merits of the literature, the language, the laws, the political institutions, and the mores that Americans have received, in the course of four centuries, from the British people. For if a civilization never is challenged, that civilization tends to sink into apathy—and slowly to dissolution.

Intellectually puny

Multiculturalism is animated by envy and hatred. Some innocent persons have assumed that a multicultural program in schools would consist of discussing the latest number of *The National Geographic Magazine* in a classroom. That is not at all what the multiculturalists intend. Detesting the achievements of Anglo-American culture, they propose to substitute for real history and real literature—and even for real natural science—an invented myth that all things good came out of Africa and Asia (chiefly Africa).

Intellectually, multiculturalism is puny—and anti-cultural. Such power as the multiculturalist ideologues possess is derived from political manipulation: that is, claiming to speak for America's militant "minorities" (chiefly those of African descent). These ideologues take advantage of the sentimentality of American liberals, eager to placate such "minorities" by granting them whatever they demand. But what fanatic ideologues demand commonly is bad for the class of persons they claim to represent, as it is bad, too, for everybody else. To deny "minorities" the benefits of America's established culture would work their ruin.

"Culture, with us, ends in headache," Ralph Waldo Emerson wrote of Americans in 1841. Should the multiculturalists have their way, culture, with us Americans a century and a half later, would end in heartache—and in anarchy. But to this challenge of multiculturalism, presumably the established American culture, with its British roots, still can respond with vigor—a life-renewing response. Love of an inherited culture has the power to cast out the envy and hatred of that culture's adversaries.

Notes

1. Jeffries it was who drafted the report "A Curriculum of Inclusion" to submit to the New York Board of Regents. During the summer of 1991, Mr. Jeffries indulged himself in denunciation of the Jews, some of them having been obstacles in his deconstructive path; his epithets opened the eyes of persons who had fancied that multiculturalism was merely an endeavor to inform the rising generation about the contributions made to American civilization by folk from many lands.

2. Published in 1949.

9

America Should Embrace Diverse Cultural Influences

Reed Way Dasenbrock

Reed Way Dasenbrock is an English professor at New Mexico State University in Las Cruces.

Contrary to the opinions of both proponents and opponents of multiculturalism, Western culture is not a single, unified entity. It is rather a consolidation of disparate cultures that evolved gradually over thousands of years as various groups imitated and influenced one another. America should neither cling to the erroneous notion of a homogeneous Western culture nor adopt an equally narrow anti-Western multiculturalism. Instead the nation should embrace a genuine multiculturalism that assimilates and syncretizes the best aspects of all of the world's cultures. This would not be a surrender of the Western tradition as much as a reaffirmation of it.

Multiculturalism in the air. The recent movement in American education—both in the schools and in colleges and universities—to incorporate into the curriculum works from non-Western cultures has aroused an exceptional amount of public debate. A cover story in *Newsweek*, long discussions in the *Atlantic* and the *New Republic*, vociferous denunciations from George Will and other conservative intellectuals, even a speech by George Bush touching on the matter—this amounts to an unusual outpouring of attention in a country very little given to debating (or even noticing) intellectual or educational issues. Perhaps it is because we are so out of practice in this matter that the terms of the debate have been so poorly defined.

Opposition to multiculturalism has come most noticeably from the right, and the terms of that opposition seem clear. Our country is part of Western civilization, and it is Western civilization that has given us what is admirable about our society: its democracy, its commitment to due process, its economic and political openness, its technology and high standard of living. The education system plays a crucial role in maintaining our commitment to these values, and we ought to teach a curriculum centered on Western culture precisely for that reason. In an effort not to seem prejudiced, most of those articulating this view add that learning

Reed Way Dasenbrock, "The Multicultural West," *Dissent*, Fall 1991. Copyright 1991 by the Foundation for the Study of Independent Ideas, Inc. Reprinted by permission.

something about other cultures is of course a good idea, but non-Western cultures are *other* cultures: our culture is Western culture.

What has not been sufficiently noticed is how the multiculturalist position shares many of the same presuppositions as this conservative critique of multiculturalism. Multiculturalists also refer to Western culture as a single unified entity; they, too, argue that the foundation of American culture is Western culture. Multiculturalism is called for because it mandates the incorporation of other cultures, the non-Western cultures, into the curriculum alongside (or in some more radical "afrocentric" versions, instead of) the Western culture that has always been taught. Thus, both positions assume that multiculturalism can come into being only by the incorporation of non-Western culture in the curriculum. The status quo ante that conservatives want to preserve, and that multiculturalists want to change, is seen by both as *monoculturalism:* a coherent, univocal entity called Western culture.

I find this a remarkable misreading of European and American history and of the nature of "Western culture." I'm not sure whether the misreading by the "defenders of the West" or by the multiculturalists is more remarkable. In any case, it is this misreading of the nature of Western culture that has allowed the discussion to become so sterile and unproductive. To pay some attention to the history of Western culture, I want to argue, makes our present situation look very different from the way it has been portrayed, far less a unique challenge to our culture (or even a unique opportunity) than another example of something we have faced and faced successfully many times before. For, when looked at with a modest effort of imaginative accuracy, Western culture is itself an example of multiculturalism.

Cultural origin and influence

This should be obvious to anyone upon a moment's historical reflection. When we speak of a common Western culture or, more narrowly, of a common European culture, we are speaking of something that took millennia to construct and consolidate. There was no common European identity two thousand years ago, just a collection of disparate peoples and cultures ranging from the world's most powerful and sophisticated, the Roman Empire, to the rude Germanic and Celtic peoples of the North. By now, it is those rude, uncivilized people who seem to stand at the center of European culture. Joseph Conrad's brilliant frame for *Heart of Darkness* reminds his British readers of 1900 that Britain, by then the very center of European civilization, was once also a "heart of darkness," considered by its Roman conquerors to lie at the outer edges of civilization.

What created the relative coherence of European culture we see today out of this multiplicity of peoples, cultures, and traditions? Contemporary thinking usually answers, *domination*—assuming that we always go on being ourselves until someone else overpowers us. However, though force undoubtedly played a role, Europe did not take shape primarily through conquest or forcible assimilation. (The Roman Conquest of Britain left a few ruins but had little lasting effect.) It was created primarily by cultural imitation, the mysterious process by which one culture responds to the influence of another. Indeed, the key moment in the creation of a European culture was not the initial sudden emergence of essential Western concepts such as democracy in Athenian Greece. It was, instead, the more gradual process by which another society— Rome—underwent Hellenization and took over Greek ideals and culture as its own. Differences remained, but cultural influence and imitation created a degree of commonality such that we can speak with some accuracy of a shared Graeco-Roman or classical civilization. Virgil thus is in a sense more important in the creation of "Western" culture than Homer precisely because of his acceptance of Homer as a normative ideal. This process of imitation, repeated many times over, gives birth to the essential Western concept that culture is not autochthonous, that it comes from somewhere else: from the East, if one is a Midwesterner or Westerner; from Europe, if one is American or Russian or Australian; from the Continent, if one is British; from the Mediterranean, if one is Nordic; from Greece, if one was Roman. Culture thus is not what we do but usually what someone else does better than we do. This relation is always double-edged: the provincial side both resents and admires the sophisticated side in the relationship. But there is never any ambiguity about which is the sophisticated side: it is, simply, the side that is the object of imitation over the long term.

> *There was no common European identity two thousand years ago, just a collection of disparate peoples and cultures.*

Now this sense of culture as something learned, something constructed, something that we share with and take from others, is in quite sharp contrast to the anthropological sense of culture as the ensemble of practices of a given community. The difference is between a normative or prescriptive and a descriptive concept. Culture in the normative sense is what we ought to do; for an anthropologist culture is what a given people do. The anthropological sense seems to govern the current use of the term among multiculturalists, particularly in their assumption that it is important to "preserve" the culture of minority students. African Americans should study African and African American literature to maintain their own cultural identity as African Americans, and it is partly for this reason that it is deemed important to have African Americans—not members of other groups—teaching these subjects. Yet the educational practice urged on the society as a whole by multiculturalists is deeply Virgilian. Multiculturalists urge members of the mainstream culture to learn about other cultures so that we can learn from them as well as learn about them. Diversity in the curriculum is seen as important because other cultures have traits to learn from; the project is for our students and our society to become more multicultural, not simply to be more informed about other cultures. And if we are to become more multicultural, then we must consciously become a combination of what we wish to retain from our culture and what we wish to adopt from that of others. We must become like Virgil. And it is for the same reason that this project is also resisted so strongly: those opposed to multiculturalism are just as Virgilian, insisting that we should model ourselves on the models we have long imitated, not on "alien" traditions and ways of being.

However, those on both sides who present Western culture and multiculturalism as if they were opposed options miss what I would call the fundamental multiculturalism of Western culture, the fact that it has been constructed out of a fusion of disparate and often conflicting cultural traditions. The straw man of the multicultural polemics is now the dead white European male or the Anglo; only twenty years ago the straw man of comparable polemics was the White Anglo-Saxon Protestant. Whatever happened to the WASP?

Culture in the normative sense is what we ought to do; for an anthropologist culture is what a given people do.

In just one generation, it would seem, the once crucial distinctions between Protestant and Catholic, between Protestant and Jew, between Anglo-Saxons and other European ethnic groups have ceased to matter: all of these groups are seen to be part of a homogeneous "eurocentric" tradition. But these internal barriers inside the "Western tradition" in America did not go away magically or easily, any more than the internal barriers inside of Europe did. One might remind anyone glibly referring to "the European tradition" (as if it were a harmonious whole) of the long conflict from 1914 to 1945 (or really from about 1500 to 1945) concerning who was to dominate Europe; one might remind anyone glibly talking about a homogeneous Anglo culture in the United States of the intense resistance, as recently as 1960, to the election of the Irish Catholic John F. Kennedy to the presidency. If we can talk about European unity or about a certain unified "Anglo" culture in this country, it is only as a result of a long historical process of knocking down the walls that have separated the different European communities. And that process is not complete even today.

The wall that multiculturalist slogans create between *just one* Western culture and non-Western culture thus reflects a kind of amnesia. Moreover, the disparate elements out of which "Western culture" has been created are themselves often non-Western in origin. One of the loci of the recent debates has been the argument advanced in Martin Bernal's *Black Athena* and elsewhere that classical Greek culture is deeply indebted to Egyptian (and therefore to "black") culture. The debate here is really about the extent to which Egyptian culture can be said to be African. For there is no disputing the obvious debt of Hellenic culture to ancient Egyptian and Near Eastern cultures. However the details of this particular controversy sort out, the imitativeness of Western culture—its ability to learn from cultures outside the West as well as from other places inside the West—has obviously been one of its constitutive features. We might broaden T. S. Eliot's dictum and say that "immature cultures borrow, mature cultures steal."

Christianity in Europe

After all, if the heritage of classical civilization is one key strand in Western culture, the second key strand would have to be Christianity. For it was really Christianity, not the classical heritage, which cemented a sense of European identity: the fundamental affirmation of European identity has come from Europeans defining themselves as Christian in opposition to cultures that were seen as heathen or pagan. Yet this is deeply paradoxical. Is Christianity a Western or European religion? Its birthplace is undoubtedly "Eastern" and non-European, and it stands in close relation to other religions seen clearly as non-Western and "other," particularly Zoroastrianism and Islam, or whose status in this cultural geography is problematic, particularly Judaism. If one master concept could be said to crystallize a Western mind-set, it is probably not democracy—which so many European countries managed to do without for so long—as much as monotheism. Monotheism allowed us to justify conquest of the "pagan" and "idolatrous" countries of the non-Western world; it also, by removing the sacred from the natural world to a metaphysical realm, justifies thinking of the natural rwerld as something to be used, transformed, and conquered. Yet monotheism is an indigenous notion nowhere in Europe. It was introduced to Europe by Christianity, but derived immediately from Judaism, and ultimately from Zoroastrianism. This helps to explain why, if classical civilization and Christianity are the two most important strands or constitutive elements of Western culture, it took an immense synthesizing labor across centuries to bring them into some sort of harmony. Dante, Spenser, and Milton—in seeking to fuse classical culture with Christianity—are thus in a sense just as multicultural as Virgil was, and if we fail to realize this immediately, we are only testifying to how successful their work of assimilation was.

Science and technology

Finally, the third key element in any definition of Western culture would have to be science and technology. This is crucial both for the monoculturalist praise of the West (Jacob Neusner's insistence that "we are what the rest of the world wants to be") and the multiculturalist critique, which tends to find in other cultures a saner because more respectful attitude towards nature. Yet Western science and technology (whether we think it a good or a bad thing) is no more exclusively Western than Western religion. Even if much of it comes from the Greeks, they took their astronomy from the Sumerians and Egyptians, and we only know about much of Greek science because of the Arab role in transmitting it. It is hard to imagine "Western" science without the Chinese invention of gunpowder, rockets, and printing, without the Indian and Arab contributions to mathematics, and without the key Arab discovery of how to sail upwind.

Consider, for a final example, the "Western calendar," now sometimes resisted for imposing a common "eurocentric" grid on the world. How many elements enter into a date such as Thursday, August 15, 1991? The name of the day comes from a Norse God, the name of the month from a Roman emperor. The year comes (approximately) from the date of Christ's birth, so is Christian in inspiration, but the numerical system is Arabic (and ultimately Indian) in inspiration. Nor is this hybridization and syncretism anything uniquely Western. For many of the world's central cultures are multicultural in the sense I am describing, made up of complex mixtures of local and borrowed elements. Even when we can find someone located univocally in what seems to be a homogeneous culture, a historical perspective shows how that culture was itself formed at some earlier point out of a multicultural context. The way in which successive European cultures rewrote the Homeric epics to trace their own history back to Greece is paralleled by the successive rewriting of the Indian epics, the *Mahabharata* and the *Ramayana*, in Southeast Asia. Indian culture is a complex mixture of indigenous Hindu and imported Muslim elements, and Islam has been a profound influence on the culture of much of Africa. Our current models of culture all seem to be either/or (eurocentric vs. afrocentric, Western vs. non-Western, monocultural vs. multicultural), but culture itself is both/and, not either/or. Multiculturalism is simply the standard human condition.

Now, nothing I have said so far should be controversial. I have recalled some basic historical facts. Yet the facts should lead us to see the debate about multiculturalism in an unexpected light. The choice cannot be between a closed Western tradition and openness to other non-Western traditions, for the Western tradition itself has always been open—if not always prone to admit that it is—to other cultural traditions. If you changed into or out of pajamas, took a bath, brushed your teeth, or had a cup of tea or coffee this morning, each of these activities is something we have taken from Asia. If, say, William Bennett's attitudes toward other cultures had always been dominant in the West, we would still be worshipping Zeus and trying to use Roman numerals. The very spirit of the West when it encounters another cultural practice is to say, "Is there something we can use here?" Is tobacco good to smoke? Is coffee good to drink? Is chocolate good to eat? Not every borrowing has been wise, but by and large Western culture has been immeasurably enriched by its ability to adapt to and borrow from others.

If this history teaches us anything, it is that crises of multiculturalism have deep historical roots and cannot be wished away. Early mediaeval England was a country riven by a schism between the indigenous culture and language of the Anglo-Saxons and the imported culture and French language of the conquering Normans: what resulted was the hybrid language of English and a profoundly hybrid and syncretic culture. Multiculturalism has emerged in the United States today out of a comparable historical exigency. On the one hand, we are faced with a new wave of immigration into the United States: our country is becoming less European, less white, more Asian and more Latin American. Europe, having for decades felt smug and superior about racial problems and tensions in America, is faced with the same phenomenon and is—if anything—considerably less prepared to deal with it. On the other hand, we and every other trading nation are faced with an increasingly integrated world, above all an increasingly integrated international economy, in which we can no longer pretend to separate ourselves from other nations. Borders are now gates, not walls, through which pour problems—drugs and too many Toyotas—but also essential ingredients such as oil. Most important, across borders now pour people. And each of these tendencies is likely to become more pronounced, not less, for the foreseeable future. How do we respond to the complex interaction of cultures that shapes the contemporary world?

Keeping the best

My answer may seem paradoxical: we need to adopt a good deal of the multiculturalist agenda precisely because it is in keeping with the best and most important aspects of Western and American culture. The great moments of our historical tradition have been moments of contact with and borrowing from other cultures: a good deal of what was important about the Middle Ages was prompted by contact with Islamic civilization; Greek exiles in Italy helped spark the Renaissance, as did the discovery of the New World; the discovery of the spiritual traditions of Asia played an important role in British and particularly American Romanticism. Our historical situation is perhaps more complex than any of these, since we are now in contact with the entire world through immigration and trade, but it is nevertheless a situation these examples will help us to understand. When faced with disparate cultures in contact (which usually means conflict), the successful response has always been assimilative and syncretic, to mix and match, taking the best of each. We now need to do this with the totality of the cultures of the world. But this doesn't represent a surrender of the Western tradition as much as a reaffirmation of it.

It was really Christianity, not the classical heritage, which cemented a sense of European identity.

If this is what we need to do, how can we do it responsibly? Once we see the fundamental continuity between multiculturalism today and earlier moments in our history, the polemical anti-Western thrust of much multiculturalist rhetoric seems absurdly out of place, as does that side of multiculturalism seeking to "preserve" the culture of minority students by focusing their curriculum on their own culture. It is empty posturing to pretend to choose non-Western culture over Western culture when our task is to harmonize them and choose the best of both. To see the choice as one between eurocentrism and afrocentrism is to deny the very possibility of multiculturalism. The afrocentric curriculum being advocated by some black intellectuals and implemented in some school systems is both impractical and no more multicultural than the suggestions of William Bennett and George Will. Moreover, this way of framing the issue ignores the degree of acculturation already undergone by minorities in this country. Most African Americans are no more culturally African than I am culturally German.

In any case, the thought of what could happen when hundreds of thousands of not very well-informed—even if well-intentioned—school teachers and college professors are turned loose on the cultures of the world is enough to make anyone cringe, and certainly what passes for multiculturalism in the nation's schools is often shallow, misinformed, and intellectually shoddy. In kindergarten, my son brought home some nationally disseminated materials about Columbus Day that made an attempt (obviously influenced by multiculturalism) to show something about pre-contact Native American culture as well as the usual stuff about the *Niña*, the *Pinta*, and the *Santa Maria*. But the worksheet identified Columbus as landing in Bermuda, not the Bahamas; when I pointed this out to his teacher, she asked me what the difference was. This year in first grade, a whole section on Native American culture followed, so rife with misinformation and clichés that the children wouldn't have been much worse off just playing cowboys and Indians. I would be astonished if the new afrocentric schools conveyed a much more accurate sense of what African culture is really like. The point here is that even the best intentions are not enough, that misinformed teaching can in fact reinforce the stereotypes and prejudices it is attempting to move beyond. Moreover, given the spirit of guardianship for these cultures dominating the attempts to represent them in the curriculum, it is unlikely that anything but a sanitized, idealized portrait of these cultures could emerge, even though it is precisely such a portrait of Western culture that multiculturalism objects to.

English language and a world culture

So a responsible and responsive multiculturalism is not going to take shape overnight. We are in for a period of experimentation, and we can only hope that more complex models and pedagogies slowly emerge and replace the simplistic visions and responses of both sides in the current debate. To anyone searching in the interim for what such a multiculturalism would look like, my advice is to read contemporary non-Western literature written in English, which seems to me to be a crucial site where we can move toward a more sophisticated sense of the world's cultures. English is an international language, playing an important role inside about one fourth of the world's one hundred and sixty countries, and it has therefore become an important international literary language. Important—great—writing is being done in English all over the world, on every continent today. But this body of literature has not yet played an important role in the curriculum at any level, since it doesn't seem English or American enough to make it into the English curriculum, or "different enough" to make it into those parts of the curriculum concerned with other cultures. In this context, that is precisely its virtue. The writers themselves are often attacked from both sides, precisely because they don't fit into one camp or the other, as the case of Salman Rushdie has shown most spectacularly. In fact, the discussion about "afrocentricity" took shape first in literary criticism when critics such as Chinweizu attacked Wole Soyinka and other African writers for their "euromodernism." Yet the bridges these writers are building, by importing European forms into non-European contexts and by introducing non-European cultural traditions into European languages, may in retrospect seem as crucial to the formation of a world culture as the Augustan imitation of Greek culture was for the formation of classical culture and the Renaissance imitation of those classical forms and of Italian culture was for the construction of European culture.

Multiculturalism is simply the standard human condition.

I believe the construction of a world culture—as [authors] Wyndham Lewis said over forty years ago and V.S. Naipaul has recently reiterated—is the task that now faces us. Despite the fashionable nostalgia for pockets of difference yet unintegrated into a world community, the alternative to such a world culture is not a lively diversity of cultures as much as unending conflict among them. Will pointing this out magically transform the current debate into a less shrill one? Of course not, for there are powerful reasons why each side in this debate wants not to understand the other. On the one hand, advocates of a separatist cultural identity for minorities reserve their harshest criticism for those of their own communities like Naipaul or Richard Rodriguez who insist that a measure of assimilation is inevitable, that accommodation must be a two-way street. Ayatollah Khomeini's condemnation of Salman Rushdie is the most conspicuous exemplification of this rage: that one of "us" could be "polluted" by contact with the other side. On the other hand, a George Will or a William Bennett finds it hard to admit that the West might have something to learn from as well as something to teach the rest of the world.

My point is not just that both sides hold to blindingly narrow ideals. It is rather that neither side perceives the world in which we live. Despite all of the talk on both sides about preserving earlier cultural identities, these identities are changing quickly and inexorably. It is in this sense that—despite the apparent polarization of the debate—the two sides are really one. Together, they represent a point of view that is historically irrelevant.

10
Visions of a Postethnic America

David A. Hollinger

David A. Hollinger is a history professor at the University of California at Berkeley.

America was modeled as a universalist nation—one that would provide benefits of citizenship irrespective of ancestry. However, America failed miserably to act on its universalist aspirations and experienced profound inequality based on ethnicity. American society today can be regarded as consisting of five basic demographic blocs: Euro-American, Asian-American, African-American, Latina/o, and Native American. Euro-Americans, who were traditionally subcategorized into distinctive ethnic groups, are now amalgamated into one group. Similarly, fainter lines now distinguish ethnic subgroups in each of the five blocs, but the blocs themselves are divided by thicker lines. In the ideal of a "postethnic" America, these lines would be diminished, more like the lines internal to each bloc. Americans would have greater freedom to exercise their "ethnic option" of affiliating or disaffiliating with various ethnic groups.

If Alex Haley had carried out on his father's side the genealogical inquiry reported in *Roots*, he would have experienced his great moment of self-knowledge in Ireland, not Gambia. This observation was made by Ishmael Reed in the course of a symposium entitled, "Is Ethnicity Obsolete?"[1] Haley's choice of roots and Reed's comment on it together constitute an emblem for three points this viewpoint addresses. The United States is endowed with a *non-ethnic* ideology of the nation. It is possessed by a predominantly *ethnic* history. It may be now squandering an opportunity to create for itself a *postethnic* future in which affiliation on the basis of shared descent would be voluntary rather than prescribed.

The national ideology is "non-ethnic" by virtue of the universalist commitment—proclaimed in the prevailing constitutional and political discourse—to provide the benefits of citizenship irrespective of any ascribed or asserted ancestral affiliations. This commitment lies behind our sense that Haley had a real choice, and one that was truly his to make: in-

David A. Hollinger, "Postethnic America," *Contention*, Fall 1992. Reprinted with permission.

dividual Americans are to be as free as possible from the consequences of social distinctions visited upon them by others. Yet the decision Haley made was driven by a history predominantly "ethnic" in the extent to which each American's individual destiny has been determined by ancestrally-derived distinctions flagged, at one time or another, by such labels as Negro, Jewish, Indian, Caucasian, Hispanic, Oriental, Irish, Italian Chinese, Polish, white, black, Latino, Euro-American, Native American Chicano, and African-American.[2] That any person now classified as "black" or "African-American" might see his or her own life as more the product of African roots—however small or large a percentage of one's actual genealogy—than of European roots reflects this history.

Hence "Haley's Choice" comes close to being the "Hobson's Choice" of genealogy in America. Haley could choose to identify with Africa, accepting, in effect, the categories of the white oppressors who had determined that the tiniest fraction of African ancestry would confer one identity and erase another, or, Haley could choose to identify with Ireland, denying, in effect, his solidarity with the people who shared his social destiny, and appearing to wish he was white. The nature of this "choice" is illuminated by an experience reported by Reed, who shares Haley's combination of African and Irish ancestry and who has flirted with the other option in the structured dilemma I am calling "Haley's Choice": Reed mentioned his "Irish-American heritage" to a "Professor of Celtic Studies at Dartmouth," who "laughed."[3]

Postethnic America

A "postethnic" America is one in which someone of Reed's color could comment casually about his Irish heritage without our finding it a joke. A postethnic America would offer Haley a choice more real than the one Hobson offered visitors to his livery. But the notion of postethnicity entails more than this. To clarify this ideal, and to explore its prospects in the context of the nation's non-ethnic ideology and its ethnic history, is the chief concern of this viewpoint.[4]

Any such enterprise must begin by underscoring the inequalities that have dominated the historical record, and by recognizing that these inequalities now lend credibility to claims made on behalf of communities defined by descent. Not every citizen's fortune has been influenced to the same degree, or in the same direction, by America's notorious failure to act on its universalist aspirations. Being classified as Euro-American, white, or Caucasian has rarely been a basis for being denied adequate employment, housing, education, or protection from violence. One response to the patently unequal consequences of ethno-racial distinctions has been to invoke and sharpen the nation's official, Enlightenment-derived commitment to protect all its citizens from any negative consequences of ethno-racial distinctions. What this commitment means has been contested, of course, from the day a committee of the Second Continental Congress deleted from the Declaration of Independence Thomas Jefferson's denunciation of slavery right down to the most recent decisions of the Supreme Court concerning the limits of affirmative action. The commitment is plain enough, however, to make obvious the gap between the theory and the practice of American nationality.[5] Indeed, the magnitude and persistence of this gap have inspired a second, very different response: the applying of pressure from the gap's other side, its ethnic side.

This alternative strategy for closing the gap asks public authorities to facilitate and actively support affiliation on the basis of ancestry. By promoting the development of communities defined by descent, one might reasonably hope for more equal treatment of every descendant of every "tribe." After all, the results produced by the long-preferred method of gap-closing—the invoking and sharpening of the non-ethnic ideological tradition—remain disappointing even to most people who believe progress has been substantial. Hence the non-ethnic character of the ideological tradition can be construed as part of the problem, rather than part of the solution. That tradition treats as irrelevant to citizenship the very distinctions that, in this view, need to be asserted, reinforced, and celebrated.[6] This feeling that equality's interests demand for America a future even more ethnic than its past is reflected in much of what is said in the name of "multiculturalism."

Yet "multiculturalism" sometimes functions as a shibboleth behind which are concealed a range of initiatives often not in agreement about just how much ethno-racial particularism is wise. The debate over multiculturalism is often scripted as a two-sided confrontation, but it has generated a number of distinctions, refinements, and possibilities that get missed when participants characterize each other as separatists or as defenders of Eurocentric domination, and when they construct the issue as a choice between similarity or difference, wholeness or fragmentation, assimilation or dissimilation, monism or pluralism.[7] No doubt these terms describe fairly some participants in this debate, and some of the doctrines advanced, but not all. A convenient example of a perspective not encompassed by these familiar dichotomies is a 1992 essay by the historian Gary B. Nash.

A postethnic perspective challenges the right of one's grandfather or grandmother to determine primary identity.

Nash defends multiculturalism, which in the context of American historical studies he takes to be an emphasis on cultural diversity, an elimination of ethnocentrism, and the "integration of the histories of both genders and people of all classes and racial or ethnic groups."[8] Indeed, Nash is the author not only of scholarly works that manifest these ideals; he is, in addition, the principal author of the widely-discussed series of textbooks recently adopted by most public school districts in California, designed explicitly with these multicultural goals in mind.[9] Yet Nash is resoundingly critical of the Afrocentrism that is sometimes counted as a version of multiculturalism, and he mocks the ethnocentric reasoning by which our schools might be asked to design "Sinocentrist," "Khmercentrist," and "Hispanocentrist" curricula, and to ignore the needs of "mixed-race children in a society where . . . interracial marriage is at an all-time high." Nash defends the idea of "common ground" as routinely invoked by critics of multiculturalism. "If multiculturalism is to get beyond a promiscuous pluralism that gives everything equal weight and adopts complete moral relativism," says Nash in words that might have come from Diane Ravitch, Arthur M. Schlesinger, Jr., or even William Bennett, "it must reach some agreement on what is at the core of American culture."[10]

Moreover, Nash is forthright in telling us what we should take as that "core": the democratic values "clearly stated" in the nation's "founding documents." These old principles "are a precious heritage" endowing with the same rights all "individuals" of "whatever group attachments." Nash thus invokes the non-ethnic ideological tradition, identifies himself with one of this tradition's greatest defenders, Gunnar Myrdal, and points to that tradition's helpful role in "virtually every social and political struggle carried out by women, religious minorities, labor, and people of color." Scorning the varieties of particularism that encourage young people to identify only with antecedents of their own ethno-racial category, Nash insists that "Harriet Tubman and Ida B. Wells should inspire all students, not simply African-American females," and reminds us that W. E. B. Dubois once "wed" a color-neutral "Truth," and sought to "live above the veil" of color by learning from Aristotle and Shakespeare. Nash several times invokes "cosmopolitanism," a concept that matches his ideas more comfortably than does the more ambiguous "multiculturalism" with which he, like so many other opponents of an Anglo-Protestant curriculum and public culture, finds himself saddled.[11]

Cosmopolitanism and pluralism

"Cosmopolitanism" should be sorted out from several other persuasions and counter-persuasions that sometimes get confused in the multiculturalism debates. Part of the confusion derives from the fact that virtually no one defends "monoculturalism," with the result that multiculturalism is deprived of an honest, natural opposite. "Eurocentrism" is often said to be the enemy, but this word is more an opprobrious epithet than a fair description of any but a few of the people who have expressed concerns about fragmentation and loss of pedagogic focus.[12] And many who do uphold European traditions insist that what makes these traditions worth defending is their decidedly multicultural character.[13] Hence the "opponents" of multiculturalism sometimes end up seeming to claim its banner for their own, apparently different programs.[14] Another alleged opposite of multiculturalism is "universalism," but here the highly problematic claim that a given, single culture is good enough for the entire globe is often conflated with more modest assertions that some truths and rights apply to every member of the species, and that all the world's peoples share a destiny sufficiently common to demand mutual engagement and cooperation.[15] These assertions can be consistent with multiculturalism unless the latter is understood—as it sometimes is—as a mere multiplicity of ethnocentrisms. Universalism's suspicion of enclosures is shared by "cosmopolitanism," which is defined by an additional element not essential to universalism itself: recognition, acceptance, and eager exploration of diversity. Cosmopolitanism urges each polity and each individual to absorb as much experience as it can while retaining its capacity to function as a unit. Although this ideal is attractive to many adherents of multiculturalism, the latter notion's amorphousness obscures a crucial distinction between cosmopolitanism and "pluralism."[16]

"Pluralism" differs from cosmopolitanism in the degree to which it endows with privilege particular groups, especially the communities that are well established at whatever time the ideal of pluralism is invoked. While cosmopolitanism is willing to put the future of every culture at risk through the critical, sympathetic scrutiny of other cultures, and is willing to contemplate the creation of new affiliations, pluralism is more concerned to protect and perpetuate particular, existing cultures.[17] In its extreme form, this conservative element in pluralism takes the form of a bargain: "You keep the acids of your modernity out of my culture, and I'll keep the acids of mine away from yours." If cosmopolitanism is casual about community-building and community-maintenance, and tends to seek voluntary affiliations of wide compass, pluralism promotes affiliations on the narrower grounds of shared history and is quicker to see reasons for drawing boundaries between communities. Cosmopolitanism is more oriented to the individual, whom it is likely to understand as a member of a number of different communities simultaneously, while pluralism is more oriented to the group, and is likely to identify each individual with reference to a single, primary community. Cosmopolitanism is more suspicious than is pluralism of the potential for conformist pressures within the communities celebrated by pluralists, while pluralism is more suspicious than is cosmopolitanism of the variousness and lack of apparent structure in the wider world celebrated by cosmopolitans. Arguments offered by universalists that certain interests are shared by many groups will get a longer hearing from cosmopolitans than from pluralists, who are more likely to see in such arguments the covert advancement of the interests of one, particular group. Pluralism and cosmopolitanism have often been united in the common cause of promoting "tolerance" and "diversity," and thus both are strong ideological tributaries feeding the multiculturalism of our own time. But a tension between pluralist and cosmopolitan tendencies runs throughout the multiculturalist debate, and is rarely acknowledged.

A postethnic perspective

Cosmopolitanism is worth singling out because its renewal in the context of the debate over multiculturalism can yield what I want to call a "postethnic" perspective. The latter is more historically specific than cosmopolitanism. *Post*ethnicity reacts against the nation's invidiously ethnic history, builds upon the current generation's unprecedented appreciation of previously ignored cultures, and supports on the basis of revokable consent those affiliations by shared descent that were previously taken to be primordial. The great pluralist Horace Kallen thought he had made a knock-down argument for the primacy of ethno-racial identities when he observed that one thing no one can change is his or her grandfather, but a postethnic perspective challenges the right of one's grandfather or grandmother to determine primary identity. Let individuals affiliate or disaffiliate with others of shared or differing descent as they choose.[18] The postethnic ideal recognizes the need for affiliations that mediate between the individual and such gross entities as the state, the economy, and the species. If this need has been often slighted by universalists—for whom the species as a whole can be community enough—the reality of this need has led some pluralists to reify ethno-racial categories and to deny the contingent, contextual character of the process of affiliation. Part of the "post" in postethnicity is the latter's acceptance of the constructed character of "races" and "ethnic groups": a postethnic perspective is willing to "problematize"—as we say nowadays—identities that unreconstructed ethnocentrists preferred to take as given.[19]

The shifting, socially constructed character of ethno-racial groups is apparent in the recent amalgamation of what were once a host of distinctive "ethnic identities" into "Euro-American," now widely seen alongside Asian-American, African-American, Latina/o, and Native American as one of the five basic demographic blocs that constitute the bulk of American society. American multiculturalism accomplished in short order a task that centuries of British imperial power could not complete: the making of the Irish indistinguishable from the English.[20] Jewish identity, too, receded in significance when all Americans of predominantly "European" stock were grouped together.[21] It is tempting to see the new system of classification as a "quintuple melting pot," replacing Will Herberg's "triple melting pot" of Protestants, Catholics, and Jews, all of whom are now grouped together as "Euro-Americans."[22]

If the new American ethno-racial pentagon, or "quintuple melting pot," serves to erase dramatically much of the cultural diversity within the Euro-American bloc, the very drama of this transformation is salutary in two respects. First, this drama is a reminder of the contingent, contextual character of the entire process by which social identities are created, perpetuated, and altered. A New Hampshire resident of French-Canadian ethnicity may learn, by moving to Texas, that he or she is actually an "Anglo." Many European immigrants of the nineteenth century did not come to see themselves as significantly "Italian" or "German" until these identities were thrust upon them by the novel demographic conditions of the United States that rendered obsolete the local identities into which they had been acculturated in Sicily and Swabia. Distinctions between Protestants, Catholics, and Jews of European extraction were once taken as seriously as are the distinctions now made between Euro-Americans and Asian-Americans. Most ironically, those from Arab countries and Iran are not, by most indexes, called Asian-Americans, but "whites," or, by transfer, "Euro-American."

Revulsion at racism is now sufficiently strong in our society to render the ideal of postethnicity worth discussing.

A second valuable consequence of the sudden transformation of a host of ethnic identities into "Euro-America" is the invitation this experience provides to recognize the comparable erasures of diversity that victimize people within the other four, pseudo-primal categories. The tribal and linguistic distinctions among Native Americans have long been lost on many non-Indian observers. The purchase one gets on Koreans, Cambodians, Chinese, Vietnamese, and Japanese by calling them all "Asian-Americans" (or, in the older usage, "Orientals") is obtained at the cost of diminishing the significance of the differences between these, and other, Americans of Asian extraction. The Hispanic, or Latina/o bloc has more linguistic cohesion than does the Asian-American or the Native American bloc, but it, too, can be broken down into subgroups defined, for example, by such points of origin as Puerto Rico, Cuba, Mexico, and El Salvador. The internal diversity of the African-American bloc may be the least striking, as measured by some indicators, but nothing illustrates more tellingly the selective suppression of diversity and the socially constructed character of these ethno-racial blocs than the historic denial, by generations of empowered whites, that they share with black Americans a substantial pool of genes. As Barbara Fields has put the point, we still have a convention "that considers a white woman capable of giving birth to a black child but denies that a black woman can give birth to a white child."[23] Hence, "Haley's Choice."

The lines of ethnicity and race

And it is choice, so highly valued by the postethnic perspective, that by its very limits within the new ethno-racial pentagon, defines it. A Cambodian-American does not have to remain so in the eyes of non-Asian-Americans, but only with great difficulty can he or she cease to be an Asian-American. So, too with Japanese-Americans or Chinese-Americans (and, as might be asked by the Euro-American auto worker from Detroit who clubbed to death the Chinese-American Vincent Chin, thinking him Japanese, "what's the difference, anyway?"). The same applies to the other blocs: Native Americans might care who is a Cherokee and who is an Kwakiutl, but outside that section of the pentagon, an Indian is an Indian. Some Euro-Americans might make a big deal of being Jewish, but from the viewpoint of many African-Americans—returning an old favor —it is the whiteness of [the] whole lot of them that counts. And so on.

The lines between the five unequally inhabited sides of the ethno-racial pentagon mark the limits of individual movement, as set by an implicit, informal concord among the most well-positioned of the people who practice identity politics in America today.[24] These several lines are not resistant in exactly the same degree to intermarriage and other types of border-crossing and category-mixing, but all are strong enough to function as "racial" as opposed to "ethnic" boundaries. Exactly where ethnicity ends and race begins has been much contested in our time, when zoologists and anthropologists have found so little scientific utility in the concept of race, and when humanists and social scientists have found so much evidence for the socially constructed character of ethnicity, of race, and even of gender. What is shown by the prominence of what I am calling the "ethno-racial pentagon," however, is that two kinds of lines are, in fact, being drawn, and widely accepted, at least for now: fainter lines distinguish the "ethnicities" found within each of the five blocs, while bolder, thicker lines render these five blocs themselves into "races," or race-equivalents.

Nowhere within the entire ethno-racial pentagon do individuals have more freedom to choose how much or how little emphasis to place on their "ethnicity"—speaking now about the identities conferred by the "faint" lines noted above—than within the Euro-American "race," or, as I would prefer to say, bloc. The ease with which Euro-Americans can affirm or ignore their ethnic identity as Italians, Norwegians, Irish, etc., has often been noted by sociologists, and was convincingly documented recently by Mary C. Waters in *Ethnic Options: Choosing Identities in America*. Many white, middle-class Americans of third- or fourth-generation immigrant descent get a great deal of satisfaction out of their ethnic affiliations, which, in the current cultural and political environment, cost them little.[25] Waters found that these "white ethnics" tended to shy away from aspects of communal life that imposed obligations and intruded on their privacy and individuality, but affirmed what Herbert Gans calls "symbolic ethnicity": a subjective "feeling" of identity, rather than the socially substantive ethnicity entailed by involvement in a concrete community with organizations, mutual commitments, and some elements of constraint.[26]

Although Waters found abundant evidence for the voluntary character of the ethnicity affirmed by middle-class whites, she also encountered the persistence, among these manifestly voluntary ethnics, of the notion that ethnicity is a primordial, biological status. Waters's subjects' denial of the voluntary character of their own ethnic identities rendered them, in turn, insensitive to the involuntary character of the ethno-racial identities of non-whites: they see a formal "equivalence between the African-American and, say, Polish-American heritages," while often denying the depth and durability of the racism that has largely constructed and persistently bedeviled the former. Waters's book is intended, in part, to liberate whites from these blindnesses, which inhibit the extending to all Americans of the freedom now experienced by middle-class whites to affiliate and disaffiliate at will. When Waters argues for such a consummation—a time when "all Americans" are equally "free to exercise their 'ethnic option'"— she upholds the ideal I am calling postethnic.[27] In such a consummation, the vividly etched lines that define the ethno-racial pentagon would be fainter, more like the lines internal to each of the five segments. An "ethnic" America, on the other hand, would be what we have already had, only more so: the lines now vivid would be underscored, and the lines now faint would become more bold. Some programs expressed in the name of multiculturalism—those deriving more from "pluralism" than from "cosmopolitanism"—proceed in this contrary, "ethnic" direction.

A framework for discussion

It would be a mistake to ask the ideal of postethnicity to do more than serve as a distinctive frame within which can take place argument and contention over the nature of American nationality and over more specific issues in social policy. It is a frankly idealistic frame, embodying the hope that the United States can be more than an empire serving as a site for a variety of diasporas and of projects in colonization and conquest. The ideal is not a blueprint, nor a set of concrete programs. Its generality is not, however, a reason to doubt its utility. The notion of "multiculturalism" is considerably less specific, yet the work we have been asking this concept to do in our national discussion of ourselves testifies to our need for sweeping concepts. We cannot do without them. When we try, someone else's sweeping concept comes into the discourse and fills the relevant space.

Among the resources available to support the ideal of postethnicity is the tradition of cosmopolitanism as found in modern American intellectual history. "It is not because of diversity that we are in trouble," nor should our goal be to "cancel" or even to "conceal" our "differences" in the interests of "uniformity," wrote one figure in this tradition, the editor of a collection entitled *Unity and Difference in American Life*. "The problem is to get along with these differences," which should be welcomed in this "endlessly varied" universe filled with "all kinds of differences" displayed in many "groups" and many "communities."[28] The book is from 1947, and the voice is that of the Columbia University sociologist Robert M. McIver. As a theorist of diversity, McIver is not superior to most of the participants in our multiculturalist debate, but his voice, if heard at today's symposia, would be conventionally harmonious on many points. Examples of the anti-provincial strain of cultural criticism cited more widely than McIver include the careers of Randolph Bourne, John Dewey, Walter Lippmann, Margaret Mead, Ruth Benedict, and Lionel Trilling, but the literature in which they are cited is a decidedly monographic one, informing little of the popular debate over multiculturalism.[29]

It would not do to insist that these intellectuals solved effectively the problems that we struggle with today,[30] nor would it do to deny that nearly all of us would find "provincial" and sexist the specific range of ideas they took up in a spirit of cosmopolitanism. Yet the vitality of a tradition of cosmopolitan aspiration among a substantial minority of Euro-American intellectuals is worth emphasizing at this multiculturalist moment, when the imperative to confront and renounce the racism and ethnocentrism within the Euro-American bloc threatens to erase from the history of that bloc the anti-racist and anti-ethnocentric voices raised from within it. If historical representation inevitably entails the selective silencing and perpetuating of specific voices from the inventory of the accessible past—as we are now reminded at every turn by our analysts of discourse as a form of power—it is in the interests of a potentially postethnic future to keep within our hearing the cosmopolitan voices that opposed some of the same evils now being fought, and that rendered the academic culture of the mid-century decades a terrain more contested than some of our current savants find it convenient to recall. Some multiculturalist programs for academic reform justify themselves by means of a slash-and-burn rendition of the intellectual and academic history of the United States (and sometimes of Europe), according to which even the relatively recent past partook of a virtually monolithic culture of Anglo-conformist domination that remained mystified and concealed until courageously exposed by the present generation of keynote speakers and deans of humanities. But the American academy's critical tradition offers contemporary egalitarians more aid than some of them have noticed; "not everybody," as the distinguished classicist Frank M. Snowden, Jr., has put the point cogently, "is a racist."[31]

Of racists there remain all too many, of course, but revulsion at racism is now sufficiently strong in our society to render the ideal of postethnicity worth discussing. Even the failure of the "Rodney King jurors " to convict the Los Angeles police officers of criminal assault should not distract us, as Orlando Patterson and Chris Winthrop have wisely cautioned, from recognizing long-term indicators that "the vestigially prejudiced majority may be changing."[32] In an age when community closure on the basis of shared descent is being sought in so many parts of the globe, the relatively open, contingent, negotiated character of American nationality renders the United States a world-historical project more conducive than are most nationalist endeavors to the development of postethnicity. Yet the idea of a postethnic America is a challenge to be met rather than a description of a reality already achieved. The latter misrepresentation is tempting when one contemplates the range and intensity of ethnic violence in Balkan Europe, the Caucasus, East Africa, India, and in many other locales throughout the world. But a misrepresentation it truly would be, and one comparable to a misrepresentation against which this viewpoint warned at the start: the confusion of the nation's actual condition—its persistently ethnic history—with its non-ethnic ideology.

The democratic-egalitarian core of that old ideology remains vital to the vision of America I am calling postethnic. The potential of democratic-egalitarian ideals to serve as a common ground for persons of diverse descent will be diminished to the extent that these ideals become "ethnicized," which is the effect of defining them as "Eurocentric" in an era when people are encouraged in many quarters to line up their culture with their genes. The routes by which "democracy" and "equality" have travelled to reach the modern United States have been overwhelmingly Anglo-American and Western European, but that need not mean that Euro-Americans of today have a greater claim on these ideals than does anyone else. Americans within the other four ethno-racial blocs need not feel the slightest pressure to reserve their enthusiasm for democratic-egalitarian ideals until such time as evidence is produced that their own ancestral group experienced libertarian moments no less portentous than the Putney Debates [on representation during the English civil war of the 1600s].

Class concerns

The jealous particularisms that fear "common ground" as a field for covert Euro-American domination are not, however, what most immediately threatens progress toward a postethnic America. Critics of "the Balkanization of America" who focus their complaints on the educational and political programs of ethno-racial "separatists" would do well to concentrate, instead, on the rigidification of the class structure.

Economic opportunities have been vital to the process by which the once-bold lines dividing the various Euro-American ethnic groups from one another have become relatively faint, but today's poor and unskilled are offered fewer, smaller opportunities for advancement than were their comparably positioned predecessors. Persons outside the Euro-American bloc who enter the American social system with strong skills and relatively high class position often flourish, even in the current political economy. Many of these individuals—as recent immigration from Korea, Taiwan, and Vietnam demonstrates especially well—respond very positively indeed to the public culture of the United States, and in their behavior approximate the classic pattern of a certain amount of "enclaving" and a certain amount of "assimilation." If all citizens of the United States had a reasonable hope of attaining the standard of living associated with "the middle class," the prospects for a postethnic America at this point in history—when so many energies are deployed against racism—would be encouraging. But the opportunity of the United States to create for itself a postethnic future may well be squandered through its own refusal to address the needs of its poor and unskilled citizens of all ethno-racial blocs.

Notes

This essay has been influenced by the University of Michigan's Faculty Seminar on the Genealogy and Geography of Affiliation, Winter 1992. I wish to thank these colleagues for their vigorous discussions of the problem of "affiliation" in world-historical perspective. I owe special debts to Alexander Aleinikoff, Kenneth DeWoskin, Don Herzog, and Earl Lewis. I am also grateful for the many helpful comments by an audience responding to a draft of this essay presented to the Annual Meeting of the American Council of Learned Societies, Chicago, May 1, 1992.

1. Ishmael Reed, et al., "Is Ethnicity Obsolete?" in Werner Sollors, ed., *The In-*

vention of Ethnicity (New York: Oxford University Press, 1989), p. 227, commenting on Alex Haley, *Roots: The Saga of an American Family* (New York: Dell, 1976). Reed does not take the position that ethnicity is obsolete; on the contrary, he argues (229) that "ethnicity will never become obsolete" in the United States so long as "public attitudes" tend to type as "black" anyone with the slightest apparent African ancestry, and to associate with "Black America" many problems common to the society as a whole.

2. I confine this list to labels understood to be neutral or honorific. But the ethno-racial map of American society owes much to a dynamic of contempt, including the colloquial, hate-speech epithets that correspond to these socially accepted labels.

3. Reed, in Sollors, *Invention*, p. 229.

4. This essay elaborates on the argument of my "How Wide the Circle of the We? American Intellectuals and the Problem of the *Ethnos* Since World War Two," in Ronald G. Walters, ed., *Science and Social Reform in Modern America* (Baltimore: The Johns Hopkins University Press, 1993). There, I sketch the movement from species-centered to *ethnos*-centered discourse in American thought during the last several decades, and outline a "postethnic perspective" on epistemic, moral, and political communities. The concept of "postethnic" became known to me through the writings of Werner Sollors.

5. In speaking of American nationality, I do not mean that virtually everyone was a liberal egalitarian "in theory" and only choked when it came time to put the theory "into practice." The "theory" itself was often contested by people who preferred more narrowly communitarian and ethno-racially homogeneous visions of nationality. Regarding efforts to move the theory of American citizenship in "ethnic" directions, see Rogers M. Smith, "The 'American Creed' and American Identity: The Limits of Liberal Citizenship in the United States," *Western Political Quarterly* 41 (1988): 225-251.

6. The non-ethnic national ideology is sometimes said to suppress "difference" in the interest of "sameness," but this misses the real issues: What kind of difference? What kind of sameness? And for what purpose might a difference be suppressed? No one now says that ancestral differences should be considered in deciding which citizens vote, but our refusal to consider such differences is certainly an example of the suppression of difference.

7. Defenders of multiculturalism have complained with reason that critics have lumped together a range of distinctive ideas; but their next step is all too often to sweep all critics of multiculturalism into a single reactionary, establishmentarian group. A striking example of this is Evan Carton, "The Self Besieged: American Identity on Campus and in the Gulf," *Tikkun* 4 (July/August 1991): 40-47, which characterizes as "Operation Campus Storm" criticisms of multiculturalism and attacks on "political correctness" published in *Time*, *Newsweek*, the *New Republic*, and *Atlantic*. Carton links these to "Operation Desert Storm" in the Gulf, and treats as a fair emblem for this George Will's praise for Lynne Cheney as our "secretary of domestic defense." For a sharply contrasting mode of response see Louis Menand, "Illiberalisms," *New Yorker* (May 20, 1991): 101-107, in which Menand dares to acknowledge—amid a scorching and effective critique of Dinesh D'Souza's *Illiberal Education* (New York: Free Press, 1991)—that some of what is said in the name of multiculturalism is pretty silly, and implies that we should not shrink from saying so for fear

of being linked with the Far Right.

8. Gary B. Nash, "The Great Multicultural Debate," *Contention*, I, 3 (Spring 1992): 11.

9. See the three books, for different grade levels, by Beverley J. Armento, Gary B. Nash, Christopher L. Salter, and Karen K. Wixson, all by Houghton-Mifflin (Boston, 1991): *From Sea to Shining Sea, America Will Be,* and *A More Perfect Union.* Based on a selective reading of these books, I believe they do fulfill the goals of multiculturalism as Nash defines it. These books devote extensive and sympathetic attention to a great variety of American ethno-racial groups, and interpret the major episodes in the history of British North America and the United States in terms that are refreshingly consistent with the anti-racist scholarship of professional historians during the past generation.

10. Nash, "Debate," 22, 24. Diane Ravitch, "In the Multicultural Trenches," *Contention*, I, 3 (Spring 1992), distinguishes as sharply as does Nash between Afrocentrism and multiculturalism, and pleads for the recognition of commonalities amid easily distinguished cultural diversities. See also Ravitch, "Multiculturalism," *American Scholar* 59 (1990): 337-354, and Arthur M. Schlesinger, Jr., *The Disuniting of America: Reflections on a Multicultural Society* (New York: Norton, 1992). I do not mean to slight the differences between Nash, on the one hand, and Ravitch and Schlesinger, on the other. Nash is more deeply critical of the interpretations of American history and culture that prevailed before the multicultural enthusiasms of recent years, and more insistent that ways be found to articulate and appreciate the variety of cultural traditions that have gone into the making of the contemporary United States. Yet their writings confirm that some of multiculturalism's defenders and critics are backing into one another as they recoil from the ethnocentrism of either the European or the African variety.

11. Nash, "Debate," 23, 24, 25. Nash's intervention in the multicultural debate can be compared with that of another historian, Elizabeth Fox-Genovese, "Between Individualism and Fragmentation: American Culture and the New Literary Studies of Race and Gender," *American Quarterly* 42 (1990): 7-34. See also Bruce Robbins, "Othering in the Academy: Professionalism and Multiculturalism," *Social Research* 58 (1991): 354-372, which makes a vigorous and discerning defense of "cosmopolitanism," an "unfashionable term that needs defending" (358-359). Robbins also vindicates democratic values as the desired "common project" (372).

12. The term "Eurocentric" may be fair, however, as applied to Lewis S. Feuer, who identifies "disease and massacre" as the "principal offerings" of "Central African culture," and attacks multiculturalism as "a secession from Western Civilization" comparable to that carried out by the Christian anti-intellectual sects who burned the library in ancient Alexandria. See Feuer, "From Pluralism to Multiculturalism," *Society* 29 (1991): 19-22.

13. For an agitated example of this insistence, see Reed Way Dasenbrock, "The Multicultural West," *Dissent* (Fall 1991): 550-555. Dasenbrock does not, however, disparage the study of non-European cultures; he argues (553) that "Multiculturalism is simply the standard human condition," and that it applies to Europe and the United States as a matter of course, and endows both with much of the value they have.

14. Diane Ravitch comes out foursquare for multiculturalism in her contribution to *Contention*, cited above.

15. A vivid example of a universalist pronouncement in American discourse is the great courtroom speech of Eugene Victor Debs: "So long as there is a lower class, I am in it; so long as there is a criminal element, I am of it; so long as there is a soul in prison, I am not free." These proclamations of extensive fraternity contrast with all prescriptions to look after "one's own kind."

16. I have tried to distinguish "cosmopolitanism" from "pluralism" in my *In the American Province: Studies in the History and Historiography of Ideas* (Bloomington, Ind.: Indiana University Press, 1985), p. 57, using Randolph Bourne as an exemplar of the former and Horace Kallen as an exemplar of the latter.

17. There exists a rich literature on pluralism that has gone remarkably little used in the multiculturalism debate. Especially important is John Higham, "Ethnic Pluralism in Modern American Thought," in Higham's *Send These to Me: Immigrants in American Life* 2nd. ed. (Baltimore: The Johns Hopkins University Press, 1984), pp. 198-232. A helpful overview is Olivier Zunz, "The Genesis of American Pluralism," *Tocqueville Review* 9 (1988): 201-219. See also Werner Sollors, "A Critique of Pure Pluralism," in Sacvan Bercovitch, ed., *Reconstructing American Literary History* (Cambridge, Mass.: Harvard University Press, 1986), pp. 250-279, with its provocative interpretation of Horace Kallen, the most prominent theorist of "cultural pluralism" in the United States.

18. The partial reconfiguration of the discourse over "race" and "ethnicity" into the terms "descent" and "consent" has been a contribution of Werner Sollors, *Beyond Ethnicity* (New York: Oxford University Press, 1986).

19. A recognition that ethno-racial groups are constructed in contingent circumstances, and shift their boundaries according to context, is a major theme in recent scholarship. Alexander Nehamas summarizes the implications of this scholarship in a recent challenge to Richard Rorty, "when the very idea of one's *ethnos* is being put everywhere into question how can one be 'ethnocentric'?" See Nehamas, "A Touch of the Poet," *Raritan* 10 (1990): 113.

20. This point is made by the journalist Bob Callahan in a clever account of a decision by the California Arts Council concerning who was and was not a "minority"; see Callahan in Sollors, *Invention*, 232.

21. "So much for the distinctiveness that has enlivened our souls for three millennia," complains Arnold Eisen on behalf of Jews, "and, again recently, led to the destruction of our bodies." See Eisen, "University Truths," *Tikkun* 6 (1991): 55. But cf. Walter P. Zenner, "Jewishness in America: Ascription and Choice," in Richard D. Alba, ed., *Ethnicity and Race in the U.S.A.: Toward the Twenty-First Century* (New York: Routledge, 1988), pp. 117-133, which addresses the diminished distinctness of the Jewish population within the Euro-American bloc, regardless of what perspective may be brought to the issue by members of other blocs.

22. Will Herberg, *Protestant-Catholic-Jew: An Essay in American Religious Sociology* (Garden City, N.Y.: Doubleday, 1955).

23. Barbara J. Fields, "Ideology and Race in American History," in J. Morgan Kousser and James M. McPherson, eds., *Region, Race, and Reconstruction* (New York: Oxford University Press, 1982), p. 149.

24. Although this ethno-racial pentagon is now in vogue, it is not the only demographic map being advanced. One prominent competitor centers on "people of color," which implies a bi-polar construction. In this view,

white and non-white are the two relevant categories, and all distinctions between the various "colored" peoples are less significant than their being non-white. The greater acceptance of the ethno-racial pentagon is indicated by the frequency with which one is asked to identify oneself in terms of this pentagon on application forms, on health-care questionnaires, and on other forms.

25. Mary C. Waters, *Ethnic Options: Choosing Identities in America* (Berkeley: University of California Press, 1990), p. 147. See also Richard D. Alba, "The Twilight of Ethnicity Among Americans of European Ancestry: The Case of the Italians," in Alba, ed., *Ethnicity and Race*, pp. 134-158.

26. Herbert Gans, "Symbolic Ethnicity in America," *Ethnic and Racial Studies* 2 (1979): 1-20, esp. 9.

27. Waters, *Ethnic Options*, 157-158, 167, 164.

28. R. M. McIver, "What We All Can Do," in McIver, ed., *Unity and Difference in American Life* (New York: Columbia University Press, 1947), pp. 152-153. This volume is an interesting document in the history of American discourse about unity and difference. See, for example, the essays by Lawrence K. Frank (33-40), E. Franklin Frazier (43-59), and Clyde R. Miller (107-118).

29. Examples of this literature include Terry A. Cooney, *The Rise of the New York Intellectuals: Partisan Review and Its Circle, 1934-1945* (Madison: University of Wisconsin Press, 1986); Thomas Bender, *New York Intellect* (New York: Knopf, 1987); Thomas Bender, "Lionel Trilling and American Culture," *American Quarterly* 42 (1990): 324-347; Richard Handler, "Boasian Anthropology and the Critique of American Culture," *American Quarterly* 42 (1990): 252-273; Leslie J. Vaughan, "Cosmopolitanism, Ethnicity, and American Identity: Randolph Bourne's 'Trans-National America'," *Journal of American Studies* 25 (1991): 443-459; and Susanne Klingenstein, *Jews in the American Academy, 1900-1940: The Dynamics of Intellectual Assimilation* (New Haven: Yale University Press, 1991).

30. One feature of this earlier discourse that seems significant in today's context is the struggle of Jewish intellectuals to work out an orientation toward Jewish identity consistent with their identity as Americans and as cosmopolitans.

31. As quoted by Molly Myerowitz Levine, "The Use and Abuse of *Black Athena*," *American Historical Review* 98 (1992): 440.

32. Orlando Patterson and Chris Winthrop, "White Poor, Black Poor," *New York Times*, May 3, 1992, IV, 17.

Organizations to Contact

The editors have compiled the following list of organizations concerned with the issues debated in this book. The descriptions are derived from materials provided by the organizations. All have publications or information available for interested readers. The list was compiled on the date of publication of the present volume; names, addresses, and phone numbers may change. Be aware that many organizations take several weeks or longer to respond to inquiries, so allow as much time as possible.

American Civil Liberties Union (ACLU)
132 W. 43rd St.
New York, NY 10036
(212) 944-9800

The ACLU, among its many functions, champions the human rights of minorities and others as guaranteed in the Declaration of Independence and the Constitution. It defends the rights of ethnic minorities in such areas as education, housing, and immigration. The ACLU publishes public policy reports, handbooks, civil liberties books and pamphlets, and the quarterly tabloid *Open Forum*.

American Immigration Control Foundation (AICF)
PO Box 525
Monterey, VA 24465
(703) 468-2022
fax: (703) 468-2024

The foundation is an independent research and education organization that warns of the danger of massive immigration, especially illegal immigration, to America. It supports stricter measures to end illegal immigration and encourages stronger limitation of legal immigration. AICF publishes the monthly newsletter *Border Watch*, the booklets *Immigration Out of Control* and *The Path to National Suicide: An Essay on Immigration and Multiculturalism*, and the book *America Balkanized: Immigration's Challenge to Government*.

Association of Multi-Ethnic Americans (AMEA)
PO Box 191726
San Francisco, CA 94119-1726
(510) 523-2632

The association includes local organizations representing interracial and multiethnic families and individuals. It conducts educational programs and promotes the advancement of multiethnic children and adults. AMEA publishes the quarterly *Melange*.

California/National English Campaigns
3385 Arden Way
Sacramento, CA 95825
(916) 482-6175
fax: (916) 482-2045

The campaigns propose that government end its multilingual services to minorities and make English the official language. It opposes public schools' overemphasis of bilingualism and believes that all minority students should be taught in English. Each campaign publishes its own quarterly newsletter.

Center for Democratic Renewal (CDR)
PO Box 50469
Atlanta, GA 30302-0469
(404) 221-0025

CDR is a national clearinghouse for information about the white supremacist movement in general and the Ku Klux Klan in particular. It works to end racial violence and bigotry and offers programs of education, research, victim assistance, community organizing, leadership training, and public policy advocacy. Its publications include the bimonthly newsletter the *Monitor* and the manual *When Hate Groups Come to Town: A Handbook of Community Responses.*

Congress of Racial Equality (CORE)
1457 Flatbush Ave.
Brooklyn, NY 11210
(718) 434-3580

CORE is a human rights organization that works to promote civil liberties and social justice. It seeks to establish true equality and self-determination for all people regardless of race, creed, or ethnic background. Its publications include the quarterly *CORE Magazine* and the monthly newsletter the *Correspondent.*

Ethnic Anonymous (EA)
c/o F.J. Nubee
1631 Belmont Ave., #107
Seattle, WA 98122
(206) 325-8091

EA is a self-help group patterned after Alcoholics Anonymous. It applies AA's twelve-step program to individuals "whose common problem is an inability to view the self and others as equals and to maintain functional lives." EA conducts research and educational programs and publishes the quarterly *Ethnic Anonymous Newsletter.*

Federation for American Immigration Reform (FAIR)
1666 Connecticut Ave. NW, Suite 400
Washington, DC 20009
(202) 328-7004
fax: (202) 387-3447

FAIR works to stop illegal immigration and to limit legal immigration. It supports stricter enforcement of U.S. borders, efforts to prevent visa abuses, and the economic development of nations that are a source of immigration. FAIR publishes a monograph series and brochures, the periodic newsletter *FAIR Immigration Report*, the bimonthly *FAIR Information Exchange*, and other publications, including *Ten Steps to Securing America's Borders* and *Immigration 2000: The Century of the New American Sweatshop.*

The Heritage Foundation
214 Massachusetts Ave. NE
Washington, DC 20002
(202) 546-4400

The foundation is a conservative think tank that supports limited govern-ment and the free-market system. Many of its scholars and speakers oppose affirmative action, multiculturalism, and other policies and programs partial to minorities. It publishes books, monographs, speeches, and the quarterly magazine *Policy Review*.

Nation of Islam (NOI)
734 W. 78th St.
Chicago, IL 60620
(312) 602-1230

The Nation of Islam is an organization of black Muslims, led by minister Louis Farrakhan. NOI preaches black unity through the self-discipline and self-reliance of blacks. Its many functions include the operation of businesses; counseling programs for prisoners, drug addicts, alcoholics, and gang mem-bers; and a Muslim school. In many inner cities, NOI "soldiers" seek to im-prove living conditions by patrolling housing projects and neighborhoods and by deterring crime and drug dealing. Its publications include the *Final Call*, a biweekly tabloid.

National Alliance Against Racist and Political Repression (NAARPR)
11 John St., Suite 702
New York, NY 10038
(212) 406-3330
fax: (212) 406-3542

The alliance is a coalition of political, labor, church, civic, student, and com-munity organizations that oppose the many forms of human rights repression in the United States. It seeks to end the harassment and deportation of illegal immigrant workers. The alliance publishes the quarterly newsletter the *Orga-nizer* as well as pamphlets.

National Association for the Advancement of Colored People (NAACP)
4805 Mt. Hope Dr.
Baltimore, MD 21215
(212) 481-4100

The NAACP's purpose is to achieve equal rights for all and to end racial prej-udice by combating discrimination in such areas as employment, housing, the justice system, schools, and voting. The association publishes a variety of newsletters, books, pamphlets, and the monthly magazine *Crisis*.

National Association of Scholars (NAS)
575 Ewing St.
Princeton, NJ 08540
(609) 683-7878

NAS is an organization of college and university faculty members, adminis-trators, and graduate students. The association advocates the preservation of intellectual standards in scholarship and higher education. It seeks to provide students with what it believes to be the classic function of higher education: an informed understanding and appreciation of the Western intellectual her-itage. It publishes the quarterly journal *Academic Questions* and the quarterly *Update* newsletter.

National Council of La Raza (NCLR)
810 First St. NE, Suite 300
Washington, DC 20002
(202) 289-1380
fax: (202) 289-8173

NCLR is a national organization that seeks to improve opportunities for Americans of Hispanic descent. It conducts research on many issues, including immigration, and opposes restrictive immigration laws. The council publishes the quarterly newsletter *Agenda*, periodic *Backgrounders* and *Issue Briefs*, and relevant congressional testimonies and reports.

National Institute Against Prejudice and Violence (NIAPV)
31 S. Greene St.
Baltimore, MD 21201
(410) 328-5170
fax: (410) 328-7551

The institute is a national research center concerned with violence and intimidation motivated by prejudice. It conducts research, provides information on model programs and legislation, and provides education and training to combat prejudicial violence. NIAPV publishes research reports, bibliographies, and the quarterly newsletter *Forum*.

National Urban League (NUL)
500 E. 62nd St.
New York, NY 10021
(212) 310-9000
fax: (212) 593-8250

The league is a community service agency composed of civic, business, and religious leaders who aim to eliminate institutional racism in the United States and to provide services for minorities in employment, housing, welfare, and other areas. Its research department disseminates a wide range of reports and papers on topics such as racial violence and discrimination. NUL publishes the *Urban League News* quarterly.

People Against Racist Terror (PART)
PO Box 1990
Burbank, CA 91507
(213) 461-3127

PART is composed of individuals engaged in antiracist activities. It promotes freedom, equality, self-determination, and respect for all individuals through educational programs and sponsored demonstrations. It publishes the bimonthly newsletter *Turning the Tide* and many publications on the Ku Klux Klan and neo-Nazis.

Rockford Institute
934 N. Main St.
Rockford, IL 61103-7061
(815) 964-5053

The institute is a conservative research center that studies capitalism, religion, and liberty. It works to return America to Judeo-Christian values and supports traditional roles for men and women. The institute publishes the newsletter *Main Street Memorandum* and the monthly periodical the *Family in America.* Articles in its monthly magazine *Chronicles* often question immigration policy and multiculturalism.

United States Commission on Civil Rights
1121 Vermont Ave. NW
Washington, DC 20425
(202) 376-8177

The commission is a fact-finding body focusing on discrimination or denials of equal protection of the laws because of race, color, national origin, or other factors. It evaluates federal laws and the effectiveness of equal opportunity programs but has no enforcement authority. A catalog of its publications is available from the Publications Management Division at the above address.

U.S. English
818 Connecticut Ave. NW, Suite 200
Washington, DC 20006
(202) 833-0100
fax: (202) 833-0108

U.S. English is a national organization whose purpose is to promote and defend the use of English in the United States. It supports a constitutional amendment making English America's official language and programs to ensure that all residents who do not know English have the opportunity to learn. It publishes a series of monographs and the book *Learning in Two Languages: From Conflict to Consensus in the Reorganization of Schools.*

White Aryan Resistance (WAR)
PO Box 65
Fallbrook, CA 92088
(619) 723-8996

WAR is a white supremacist organization that promotes the advancement and protection of the white race in America and abroad. WAR believes that armed conflict against nonwhites is justified to protect living space, food, and the gene pool of the white race. It publishes books, cassettes, and videotapes about white supremacy and the monthly tabloid *WAR.*

Bibliography

Books

David Allen — *Fear of Strangers: And Its Consequences.* Garnerville, NY: Bennington Books, 1993.

Derrick Bell — *Faces at the Bottom of the Well: The Permanence of Racism.* New York: Basic Books, 1992.

Leo R. Chavez — *Shadowed Lives: Undocumented Immigrants in American Society.* Orlando, FL: Harcourt Brace Jovanovich, 1992.

Linda Chavez — *Out of the Barrio: Toward a New Politics of Hispanic Assimilation.* New York: Basic Books, 1991.

Ellis Cose — *A Nation of Strangers: Prejudice, Politics, and the Populating of America.* New York: Morrow, 1992.

Ellis Cose — *The Rage of a Privileged Class.* New York: HarperCollins, 1993.

James Crawford — *Hold Your Tongue: Bilingualism and the Politics of "English Only."* Chicago: University of Chicago Press, 1992.

Gerald Early, ed. — *Lure and Loathing: Essays on Race, Identity, and the Ambivalence of Assimilation.* New York: Penguin, 1993.

Howard J. Ehrlich and Fred L. Pincus, eds. — *Race and Ethnic Conflict: Contending Views on Prejudice, Discrimination, and Ethnoviolence.* Boulder, CO: Westview Press, 1994.

Hans Magnus Enzensberger — *Civil Wars: From L.A. to Bosnia.* New York: The New Press, 1994.

Nikki Giovanni — *Racism 101.* New York: Morrow, 1994.

Robert Gooding-Williams — *Reading Rodney King, Reading Urban Uprising.* New York: Routledge, 1993.

Andrew Hacker — *Two Nations: Black and White, Separate, Hostile, Unequal.* New York: Scribner's, 1992.

Douglas S. Massey and Nancy A. Denton — *American Apartheid: Segregation and the Making of the Underclass.* Cambridge: Harvard University Press, 1993.

Thomas Muller — *Immigrants and the American City.* New York: New York University Press, 1993.

Brent A. Nelson — *America Balkanized: Immigration's Challenge to Government.* Monterey, VA: American Immigration Control Foundation, 1994.

Paul Robeson Jr. — *Paul Robeson Jr. Speaks to America.* New Brunswick, NJ: Rutgers University Press, 1993.

Arthur M. Schlesinger Jr. — *The Disuniting of America: Reflections on a Multicultural Society.* New York: Norton, 1992.

Shelby Steele — *The Content of Our Character: A New Vision of Race in America.* New York: St. Martin's Press, 1990.

Ronald Takaki	*From Different Shores: Perspectives on Race and Ethnicity in America*. New York: Oxford University Press, 1987.
Jared Taylor	*Paved with Good Intentions: The Failure of Race Relations in Contemporary America*. New York: Carroll & Graf, 1992.
Cornel West	*Race Matters*. Boston: Beacon Press, 1993.

Periodicals

The American Prospect	Special section on affirmative action at the University of California at Berkeley, Winter 1993.
Roy Beck	"The Ordeal of Immigration in Wausau," *The Atlantic Monthly*, April 1994.
Bob Blauner	"Talking Past Each Other," *The American Prospect*, Summer 1992.
Lionel Chetwynd	"Are You Talking to Me?" *National Review*, August 9, 1993.
Christianity Today	"The Myth of Racial Progress," October 4, 1993.
Chronicles	Special section on immigration, June 1993.
Wanda Coleman	"Blacks, Immigrants, and America," *The Nation*, February 15, 1993.
Ruth Conniff	"The War on Aliens," *The Progressive*, October 1993.
The CQ Researcher	"Racial Tensions in Schools," January 7, 1994. Available from 1414 22nd St. NW, Washington, DC 20037.
Kathleen Deveny	"Immigrants: Still Believers After All These Years," *The Wall Street Journal*, July 12, 1994.
Howard J. Ehrlich	"Reporting Ethnoviolence," *Z Magazine*, June 1994.
Joe R. Feagin	"The Continuing Significance of Racism: Discrimination Against Black Students in White Colleges," *Journal of Black Studies*, June 1992.
Samuel Francis	"De-Americanization," *Chronicles*, September 1994.
Samuel Francis	"It's Immigration That Drives War on Culture," *Conservative Chronicle*, June 29, 1994.
William Norman Grigg	"Letter from Utah: The New Race War," *Chronicles*, April 1994.
Andrew Hacker	"'Diversity' and Its Dangers," *The New York Review of Books*, October 7, 1993.
Jeffrey Hart	"Ethnic Hatred: How America Is Different," *Conservative Chronicle*, September 7, 1994.
Joseph A. Hawkins and Carol E. Heller	"Sowing the Seeds of Racial Tolerance," *Education Week*, September 22, 1993.
Nat Hentoff	"How to Combat Tribalism in Schools," *Liberal Opinion Week*, March 28, 1994.
Steven A. Holmes	"Survey Finds Minorities Resent One Another Almost as Much as They Do Whites," *The New York Times*, March 3, 1994.

Linus A. Hoskins   "Eurocentrism vs. Afrocentrism: A Geopolitical Linkage Analysis," *Journal of Black Studies*, December 1992.

James B. Jacobs   "Should Hate Be a Crime?" *The Public Interest*, Fall 1993.

Leon Jaroff   "Teaching Reverse Racism," *Time*, April 4, 1994.

Jacqueline Jones   "Segregation Forever?" *In These Times*, August 23, 1993.

June Jordan   "A Powerful Hatred," *The Progressive*, May 1994.

Ernest W. Lefevre   "Splitting America Apart," *Vital Speeches of the Day*, December 15, 1993.

Tru Love   "What I Learned as a White Girl in a Black School," *Ebony*, September 1993.

Dale Maharidge   "Can We All Get Along?" *Mother Jones*, November/December 1993.

Salim Muwakkil   "Nationalist Movements," *In These Times*, April 18, 1994.

National Review   Special issue on multiculturalism, February 21, 1994.

Newsweek   Special issue on the immigration backlash, August 9, 1993.

Dennis Prager   "Blacks and Liberals: The Los Angeles Riots," *Current*, January 1993.

Arch Puddington   "Black Anti-Semitism and How It Grows," *Commentary*, April 1994.

Race & Class   "Black America: The Street and the Campus," vol. 35, no. 1, July/September 1993.

Joseph Raz   "Multiculturalism: A Liberal Perspective," *Dissent*, Winter 1994.

Michael Ruby   "Time to Listen Up, Citizens!" *U.S. News & World Report*, June 13, 1994.

Diana Jean Schemo   "Segregation Mars Suburban Dreams," *The New York Times*, March 17, 1994.

Richard Sennett   "The Identity Myth," *The New York Times*, January 30, 1994.

Shelby Steele   "How to Grow Extremists," *The New York Times*, March 13, 1994.

Anne Stein   "Race Relations in America: What We Really Think of Each Other," *Human Rights*, Summer 1994.

Gabriella Stern and Dorothy J. Gaiter   "Mixed Signals: Frustration, Not Anger, Guides Race Relations on a College Campus," *The Wall Street Journal*, April 22, 1994.

Clarence Thomas   "The New Intolerance," *The Wall Street Journal*, May 12, 1993.

Time   "The Rift Between Blacks and Jews," February 28, 1994.

Time   Special issue on immigration in America, Fall 1993.

Utne Reader   Special section on ethnic tribalism, July/August 1992.

Cornel West   "Learning to Talk of Race," *The New York Times Magazine*, August 2, 1992.

John Edgar Wideman   "Dead Black Men and Other Fallout from the American Dream," *Esquire*, September 1992.

Roger Wilkins   "White Out," *Mother Jones*, November/December 1992.

Alan Wolfe   "The New American Dilemma," *The New Republic*, April 13, 1992.

Index